ERIC KAPITULIK | JAKE MACDONALD

THE
PROGRAM

LESSONS FROM
ELITE MILITARY UNITS
FOR CREATING AND SUSTAINING
HIGH PERFORMANCE
LEADERS AND TEAMS

*To our teammates, both those who are and those who
are no longer with us.*

Contents

Introduction

DECEMBER 9, 1999, was almost the last day of my life, and I still get nervous when I think about it.

Ten of my Force Reconnaissance Marines and I were training for our deployment to the Persian Gulf. We were riding in the back of a helicopter, practicing maneuvers for vessel, boarding, search and seizure (VBSS) missions. Rather than coming in to a 60-feet hover over the ship we were practicing taking over, our helicopter came in too low and too fast and struck the side of the ship.

Recognizing his error, the helicopter pilot pulled on the "collective," which would typically give lift to a helicopter, but on that day, the back left wheel was stuck in the thick metal netting that surrounds many large cargo vessels. With the wheel stuck, the helicopter inverted and plunged into the Pacific Ocean. My Marines. My teammates. We were all immediately knocked unconscious.

I'm Eric Kapitulik, the Founder and Chief Executive Officer of The Program. The Program is a team-building and leadership development company that annually works with more than 150 collegiate and professional athletic teams, and corporations of all sizes. We have one mission: "Develop Better Leaders and Create More Cohesive Teams." My Program teammates and I have been doing so for more than a decade.

Achieving the Ultimate Victory

Many families, athletic teams, and corporations do well. They "win games." But many teams, whether athletic, corporate, or family, want more. They want the big prize. The championship trophy, the cover of *Fortune* magazine, the love and respect of many generations. The question they all want answered is: How do we achieve more? More from our teammates? More from our leaders? More together?

This book will provide readers, on whatever their chosen battlefield, with a road map to compete for championships. First, we will discuss what a Championship Culture is, define the Core Values that form the culture's foundation, and develop the goals and standards that reinforce our Core Values on a daily basis. We will then discuss how we create an environment where all members of the team are committed to achieving those goals and standards.

Next, we will highlight the standards to which teammates and team leaders are held and how we create—despite the discomfort all of us feel while doing so—a culture of accountability in order to achieve the best versions of ourselves and our team.

We then discuss what we must do every day of our life while preparing to be the best teammates and best team leaders that we can be, on all the teams of which we are privileged to be a part, including our most important team, our own family. Specifically, developing our physical, mental, and emotional toughness, not making excuses or letting others make them for us, and defining "hard work" and committing to it.

Finally, effective communication is key for both teammates and team leaders; no organization can achieve prolonged, sustained success without it. The final chapters review what effective communication means, how to develop it, and then how to ensure our teams carry it out.

The Program team has led men and women and made decisions when those decisions had life-and-death consequences. Like my own. . . .

Surviving a Catastrophic Crash

We awoke in a sinking helicopter, wearing 50–75 pounds of gear, weapons, equipment, and ammunition—with no oxygen and no idea how to get out of our dire situation. I fought my way through the helicopter as it sank, looking for a way to exit. Then I started to swim, and only then did I feel true fear.

When the helicopter inverted, its blades sheared off, but the engines were still turning, causing bubbles to surround us deep beneath the ocean's surface. By the time we fought our way out of the sinking helicopter, we were deep in the dark Pacific Ocean, still wearing all that very heavy gear. I don't care how mentally and physically tough we may be, none of us can hold our breath indefinitely. Eventually, your body gasps and air rushes into your lungs. But if you're deep in the ocean, salt water rushes in. My teammates and I were underwater for so long, looking for a way to exit that sinking helicopter, that by the time we started to swim, we were all drowning.

Our bodies were shutting down. Our worlds were going black. I still get scared thinking about that moment when I first started to swim, because I can still remember thinking to myself, "I *hope* I'm swimming in the right direction."

Making things even more challenging was the fact that the helicopter had hit the water with such violence that it caused a compound fracture in my leg. So when I swam in a direction that I *hoped* was the surface, while drowning, I did so using only my arms. The bones in my right leg were completely severed.

A few meters below the ocean's surface, I could see sunlight filtering through the water, and a few moments after that I was picked up by a safety boat. I had survived. Unfortunately, six of my Marines—six of my teammates—lost their lives that day.

Within one month, we had six new teammates from 1st Force Reconnaissance Company, our parent unit, volunteer to join our team and we successfully deployed to the Persian Gulf. While my teammates and I were deployed, I decided that I would raise money for a college scholarship fund for the children of my deceased teammates. To do so, I decided to compete in the world's toughest endurance events and climb the world's tallest mountains—things that I already enjoyed doing, but now I could do them for more altruistic purposes.

Since then, I have completed eight Ironman Triathlons. I have adventure-raced across the Kalahari Desert in South Africa, throughout the state of Alaska, and from the Pacific Ocean across Costa Rica to the Caribbean. I have completed the American Birkebeiner Ski Marathon and the Canadian Death Race ultramarathon, an 80-mile trail run through the Canadian Rockies. I was one of thirty finishers of the Leadville Silverman, a 50-mile mountain bike up and over six mountain passes all higher than 14,000 feet elevation, followed by a 50-mile ultramarathon up and over those same six mountain peaks the next day. I have summited five of the fabled Seven Summits, the tallest peaks on each of the seven continents. A few years ago, I stood on the summit of Mount Everest.

I am often congratulated on these "individual" accomplishments. Yet anybody who has ever accomplished similar achievements knows just how false that classification is. Nothing that we do in our life is done as an individual. Everything we accomplish is done as a member of a team, and we all fill one of two roles on those teams: teammate or team leader. Further, I am a husband to my wife and a father to my children. None of these "individual" accomplishments would have been possible without the love and support of my family and numerous other great teammates.

Privileged to Be Part of the Team

The Program Leadership Instructors are collegiate athletes, high-altitude mountaineers, Ironman Triathletes, business owners, and combat veterans. We are husbands and wives, fathers and mothers. We all share very similar personal experiences, and exactly the same professional ones working with more than 150 collegiate and professional athletic teams and corporations annually.

Program Leadership Instructors have led men and women in the world's harshest and most deadly environments, including the battlefields of Iraq and Afghanistan. They have made life-and-death decisions and have had to live with them.

Throughout this book, Program Teammate and Lead Instructor Jake "Mac" MacDonald and I will highlight some of our Program teammates' experiences, as well as those that Mac and I have been fortunate to have in our own lives. Mac and I, and our Program instructors, have developed better teammates, better team leaders, and created more cohesive teams with thousands of teams throughout North America. We have helped to ensure that those teams don't just do well, don't just "win games," but rather that they compete for championships on whatever their chosen battlefield.

This book explains how we do so, and how you can too. Each section finishes with "Action Items" and "Saved Rounds." "Action Items" are meant to help you put our advice into action, challenge you and your teammates to advance to the next level, and become the best teammate and team leader you can be.

"Saved Rounds" is a military term used to denote any bullets that military warriors have not fired during a day of shooting, but that must still be accounted for. Even if those bullets haven't been shot, they are still important. We use the term similarly at the end of every section. The information in "Saved Rounds" wasn't "fired" earlier, but it is still important.

SECTION

I

Creating a Championship Culture

CORY WATCHED IN horror as two rocket-propelled grenades streaked over his head. One impacted on the road directly in front of his lead vehicle; the next was a direct hit on his own.

U.S. Army Sergeant Aaron Wittman in eastern Afghanistan. He would be dead within five hours of this picture being taken.

Note: Photo courtesy of Duane Wittman.

1

1

The Fundamentals of a Championship Culture

THE SUN ROSE bright and clear over the Tora Bora Mountains in eastern Afghanistan on January 10, 2013, providing a surreal moment to remind them of the beauty the world can offer in the midst of a combat zone. The president of The Program Corporate, then U.S. Marine Corps Captain Cory Ross, was acting as a military adviser, attached to an Army Special Forces A-team. For months, Captain Ross had been operating with this team of Green Berets. He went everywhere they did and participated in all their operations, from meeting with village elders and providing medical services, to fighting alongside his Army teammates against Taliban forces.

That morning, they accompanied some of the Afghan local police, men they had recruited and trained to protect their own villages, on a tour of their area. They bonded and built rapport with the Afghans throughout the morning. For lunch, the Afghans slaughtered a sheep, a sign of great respect, for the American forces. While they ate, though, Cory and his teammates began receiving radio reports of multiple military-age males moving toward the village. Cory and the Special Forces soldiers tightened security, but didn't leave the village until lunch was finished, lest they insult their hosts.

Typically, military units do not like to be predictable and will not use the same roads and paths, both to and from areas, that they are operating. However, the mountainous terrain offered no other options for Cory and his teammates. They had only one possible route back to their forward operating base. Although Cory was uncomfortable taking the same roads, the mood of the unit was still optimistic. The day was peaceful, and they were proud of the progress that they, and their Afghan counterparts, had made. That peace was completely shattered as they reached a hairpin turn in the road a short distance outside the village.

To achieve success on any battlefield, at some point we must overcome adversity. Maybe not the same amount as that about to be experienced by Cory and his teammates at this hairpin turn in the road, but company cutbacks, bad calls by the referee, sick or injured players, a poor economy, or a host of other factors will challenge all of us. In those moments, despite that adversity, an organization's culture will manifest itself in that team's ability to still successfully accomplish its mission—or not.

To achieve success on any battlefield, at some point we must overcome adversity.

To ensure the former, a culture must first be defined by the leader's Core Values and embodied by talented team members. Second, the organization's best people must determine the goals and standards that daily reinforce those Core Values. It isn't enough to say that we have a culture based on family, for example, unless we can prove it every day. Our goals—and more importantly, our standards—ensure we do so. Without them, like too many organizations, we don't have a culture based on family. Instead, we have an organization that merely makes t-shirts for their company or posts "Family" signs in the lobby.

To consistently accomplish the mission on whatever our chosen battlefield, organizations must have (1) the best people, (2) goals and standards, and finally, (3) a daily commitment to holding one another accountable for achieving them (Figure 1.1).

Figure 1.1 Three Components of a Championship Culture

2

Determining "Best"

THE PROGRAM HAS one mission: develop better leaders and create more cohesive teams. We help construct world-class organizations. World-class organizations have world-class cultures, and those cultures' foundations are its "best" people.

World-class organizations have world-class cultures, and those cultures' foundations are its "best" people.

"Best", for any organization, occurs at the overlap in the Venn diagram shown in Figure 2.1. One circle represents the organization's Core Values (more on this in Chapter 3) and the other represents talent. The "best" person for any organization is one who embodies that team's Core Values, and who is also incredibly talented. In the short term, talent helps a team accomplish its mission. Its culture, as defined by its Core Values, combined with talent, ensures that team's long-term ability to do so.

In order to lay the foundation of a Championship Culture, the question we must first answer is not what we want our organizations to *stop* doing, but rather how we want them to *start* behaving. As the leader, we do this by first determining our Core Values.

One of the first lessons all Marine Corps officers are taught (although not all learn it) is never to ask our Marines to do something

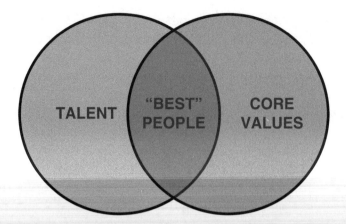

Figure 2.1 The best people for your organization have talent and share your organization's core values.

that we aren't willing to do ourselves. More importantly, don't ask them to be someone that we aren't willing to be also. It is a mistake, however, that almost all of us make. A coach tells players to clean up their messy locker room but the coach's office is even dirtier. Business leaders demand that their employees follow the organization's credit card policy, but then turn around and use their own for all sorts of questionable purchases.

Closer to home, how many parents have told their children that they need to "get outside their comfort zone," but haven't done so themselves in the past month—or the past five years?

As leaders of athletic teams, schools, businesses, and our own families, let's be better than this. We should never ask our people to do something—or more importantly, to be someone—we aren't willing to be ourselves. If we expect our team to behave in a disciplined manner (and hence one of our team's Core Values is Discipline), then as the leaders, we must behave in a disciplined manner, as well. When determining our team's Core Values, we must determine what the non-negotiable traits are that we, as the leaders, embody and expect our team to embody, as well.

Unfortunately, too many leaders make the mistake of enforcing, and then reinforcing, the behaviors they don't want, rather than asking themselves what the behaviors are that they do.

Let's not make this same mistake.

When determining desired behaviors, start by thinking about what do we, as leaders, stand for? What do we represent? What does it mean (or what do we want it to mean) to be a member of our team? The answers to these questions are our Core Values.

Parents, the head coach, or the CEO set the Core Values for the family, team, or business, respectively. We appreciate that leaders, at times, will join companies that may already have Core Values. However, if those Core Values are not already those of the new CEOs, division managers, or employees, then it will not be a good fit for the new hire, regardless of position within the organization.

However, for teams without Core Values, or for teams who realize that theirs must change, there are numerous ways to determine what their Core Values should be, and as much time as possible should be spent doing so. The following diagram and exercise illustrates one way The Program does so with our own clients.

Determining Core Values

Rick Van Arnam, former U.S. Army Colonel and principal consultant at the Table Group, first provided this exercise to us. He also offered a wealth of information surrounding Core Values, based on his work with Patrick Lencioni, who had recently published *The Advantage: Why Organizational Health Trumps Everything Else in Business* (Jossey-Bass, 2012). It should be mandatory reading for any leader.

Balance	Courage
Fitness/Physical	Knowledge
Passion	Volunteerism/Service
Structure	Growth
Fun	Efficiency
Toughness	Authority
Commitment	Discipline
Achievement	Recognition/Status
Quality	Perfection

Independence	Integrity/Trust
Legacy	Fairness
Competence	Simplicity
Wisdom	Urgency
Effectiveness	Loyalty
Accountability	Creativity/Innovation
Selflessness	Money/Wealth

1. Take three minutes and select the ten most important values to you from the list—the ten words that you feel best describe you. If a word not on the list is incredibly important to you, feel free to add it. (For example, we don't include Faith or Family for a host of reasons, but if you are compelled, please add them.)
2. Next, take one minute to narrow that list of ten down to five values.
3. Finally, take fifteen seconds to eliminate two values, leaving the top three most important or most descriptive values.

A second method of determining Core Values is simply to think about the adjectives that best describe you. Ask the people who know you best (spouse, partner, parent, best friend) to do the same for you. Ultimately, as the leader, what are the values that you embody and that you want your team to embody as well? What are the values that are most important to you?

3

Defining "Best"

ONCE WE HAVE determined our Core Values, we must then define them. The leader determines the Core Values, but at the very least, the leader, the executive team or coaching staff, and possibly a few team members whom we consider "best", should help define those Core Values.

Ray Lipsky is a friend and U.S. Naval Academy classmate of Program founder Eric Kapitulik. Ray was a member of the Navy football team and then served honorably as a Marine Corps Infantry Officer. His battalion commander, Lieutenant Colonel Paul Lefebvre, would often remind Ray, and the rest of his battalion, "Man [Woman] is a sum of his [her] experiences."

Humans are the sum of their experiences. Why is this important for our discussion on defining Core Values? Because we can't simply state that one of our Core Values is, for example, "Toughness," or that we expect our team to behave in a *tough* manner without defining what "tough" means to our organization.

The Program had the privilege to work with Coach Tom Izzo and the Michigan State men's basketball team many years ago. Michigan State is annually one of the best college basketball teams in the country and, although they do have an incredible number of very talented student athletes, they are not usually thought of as the most talented team in the country. They are known, however, for consistently being one of the toughest. Coach Izzo is tough and his team exemplifies it.

During one of our conversations with Coach Izzo, he reminded us of the importance of trying to recruit kids who are already tough and then demanding that they be tough every single day in practice. The challenge for Coach Izzo, as it is for all leaders, is that we are all a sum of our experiences.

Eric was born to Louis and Louise Kapitulik and grew up on a Christmas tree farm. His father was a Connecticut state policeman and his mother was a high school teacher. He played sports well enough that he had an opportunity to play one of them in college and was fortunate enough for that college to be the U.S. Naval Academy. He then served as a Marine Corps Infantry Officer and a Platoon Commander with 1st Force Reconnaissance Company. In his free time, he competes in the world's longest endurance events and climbs the world's tallest mountains.

He had the great fortune to have parents, and then friends and mentors, who were tough people. He did tough things and saw others doing tough things in the military and outside of it. Based on the sum of his experiences, Eric has a certain mental picture of who tough people are and what tough people do. Our teammates at The Program share very similar personal experiences. Based on all those experiences, we have our definition of tough.

This is true for everyone and their own Core Values. Based on our own life experiences, we all have a certain mental picture and a definition of those values. The members of our team may not have grown up with a dad who is a policeman and a mom who is a school teacher (or a grandfather who grew up during the Great Depression and worked in a mill his entire life). Our team members may not have grown up on a Christmas tree farm in Connecticut. As Coach Izzo highlights, our team members may have grown up with no parents, in a car, never even having a Christmas tree. By the same token, our team members may have grown up in a country club lifestyle, vacationing in Switzerland. In any case, team members have their own mental picture of tough and of what tough people do.

The Program's concept of tough may or may not be the same as that of the Michigan State men's basketball team, but if both share that Core Value, then the "best" people in both organizations must embody it. A world-class culture is founded on the "best" people. Those "best" people have talent and embody the team's Core Values. We must first select those Core Values and then define them for our team.

> *Those "best" people have talent and embody our team's Core Values. We must first select those Core Values and then define them for our team.*

4

Core Means Core!

"He who defends everything, defends nothing."

—Frederick the Great

LEADERS FROM EVERY battlefield would do well to remember this: Do not try to be everything to everyone. As Frederick the Great indicated, if we try to defend everything, we defend nothing. The Program has worked with numerous organizations whose leaders have given pushback on our belief of three (maybe four) Core Values to define an organization's culture. Their argument typically stems from their incredible success. Success affords us the opportunity to recruit almost any athlete or corporate team member that exemplifies six, seven, eight, or even twelve different values that the coach or business leader finds "important." Our response is always the same: "He who defends everything, defends nothing." Core Values are our non-negotiables. This is who we are and if you can't be it, then you can't be, and will not want to be, one of us. Another, more positive, way to say this is that our Core Values are who we are and if you are them too, then there will be no other team in the world of which you would rather be a part.

Once we have established what we believe are our Core Values, we must check to ensure that they are *core* or if we are trying to "defend everything." We accomplish this by first writing them down in a relaxed, non-stressful environment. Make your executive team, or coaching staff, do the same. If you, or they, can't readily do so, you have too many (or are doing a poor job communicating and reinforcing them, but more on these issues later).

Once you have tested yourself and your leadership team on your Core Values while sitting in a climate-controlled office, go for a run, or do anything that induces pressure or stress. Do so with your assistant coaches, team captains, or executive team. If you, or they, can't remember what your Core Values are under stress, they aren't Core.

As an example, The Program had four Core Values. Nine years ago, Program founder Eric Kapitulik was working with a women's college hockey team. During the debrief, in front of the entire coaching staff and another Program instructor, their head coach asked Eric what The Program's Core Values were. He immediately responded, "Selfless. Physical. Disciplined. And ... and ... and ..." Since that debrief, The Program has had three Core Values. (After five years in business, The Program switched Physical to Tough because we thought it was more encompassing and a more accurate representation of who we are. How we defined the Core Value didn't change, just the name of the Core Value itself.)

Determine your three or four Core Values and stand by them. There is a reason why there are three fire teams in every infantry squad and three squads in every platoon. When facing our own hairpin turns in the road, like Cory and his team just outside a village in eastern Afghanistan, our ability to remember three Core Values is slightly better than remembering four, much better than five and exponentially higher than trying to remember, as we have seen countless times, fourteen. Fourteen things may be important to us, but by definition, fourteen things can't be "Core."

5

Recruiting and Hiring "Best"

TEAMS DON'T FAIL because of lack of people. Teams fail because of who those people are. As stated earlier, Core Values define who the "best" people are for our organization, and the best people form the foundation of our culture.

Teams don't fail because of lack of people. Teams fail because of who those people are.

College and professional athletic teams spend millions of dollars annually on finding and recruiting the biggest, fastest, strongest, most talented athletes. Almost every Fortune 500 company spends even more in a never-ending search for the smartest, most talented employees. Most firms look at educational background to determine if someone might be qualified. If a recruit has the necessary talent, coaches speak to high school or AAU coaches and ask if the athlete is "a good kid." Corporate interviewers spend most of an interview asking about the applicant's extracurricular activities. This is, at best, imperfect, and for the most part doesn't at all accomplish the intended task of ensuring a good "fit." Instead, it produces favorable outcomes for individuals who share a similar personality or free-time pursuits with the interviewer.

15

The results are what you would expect: athletic teams and corporations end up with the talent they need to compete on their particular battlefield, but not the "best" people for their organization. Unfortunately, some of these same recruits are the ones who create an incredible amount of frustration and additional work for the leaders, staff, and other members of the team. Further, these very talented individuals who do not share the Core Values cause coaches and business leaders to lose their jobs, teams to fail, and businesses to close.

Instead, to assist in hiring the best people, select a group of the current "best" and task them with the added responsibility of determining "best" out of the applicant pool. Let "best" find "best." Our current best's mission during the interview, or if possible during an evaluation or "tryout" period, is to determine if an applicant exemplifies our team's Core Values.

To help prevent groupthink, we stress the importance of not discussing their opinion with other current "best" interviewers. Every team member who interviews or evaluates the new candidate will then provide their opinion of the applicant and their embodiment of our organization's Core Values. If even one of our "best" people thinks an applicant does not meet this criterion, they don't get hired. The leader then speaks to the candidate, discussing in a professional manner why they do not fit our company's culture and that it would be better for both that individual and our organization to look elsewhere.

Leaders gets more credit than they deserve when the team "does well" and more blame than they deserve when the team doesn't. This is the "responsibility of command." If we don't want that responsibility, we can still be a good player or employee, but we are no leader. Leaders enjoy the opportunity to deliver great news to the team. We must also accept the responsibility of delivering the not-so-great too!

We suggest that whichever team member would have offered employment to the applicant also be the team member to deliver the rejection. If someone has given our organization their time, then we owe it to that person to explain to them why it didn't work out.

We then repeat the process until we find a person who all our "best" people agree exemplifies our Core Values and is therefore suitable to join our organization.

Program founder Eric Kapitulik consistently tells audiences and clients that, based on the number of people he has had to fire or who didn't work out at The Program over the years, his "gut feeling" about people is not very reliable. Most of us tend to remember only the great athletic or corporate teammate for whom we "went to bat" during the hiring process and who then happened to work out great. We conveniently forget the number of very bad decisions in recruiting and hiring. Entrusting a group of our current "best" people to find other "best" applicants from a pool unfortunately doesn't guarantee hiring success, but it certainly helps.

If all our current "best" people agree that the candidate does embody our team's Core Values, the interview process is complete. The leader then tells the new applicant that everyone believes the candidate embodies the organization's Core Values, but also explains that, as president (or CEO or division head), he or she won't truly know if this is true until the candidate starts in a full-time capacity. Leaders should then require candidates to take the next 48–72 hours to decide for themselves if they embody the organization's Core Values. If they do, it will be the greatest team with whom they could work, and they will have a wonderful experience. If they do not, it will be a very bad relationship and an even worse experience for both parties. We also explain in detail that after hiring, if they do not embody our Core Values, we will decide for them, perhaps within days of their joining the team.

Hiring is an imperfect science. Regardless of the process, mistakes will still be made in whom we recruit and hire. Leaders compound that mistake by living with that hire for any period longer than the day they know a person is hurting their culture. As Mike Zak, a former Marine and current partner at Charles River Ventures (an incredibly successful venture capital firm), pointed out to his good friend Eric years ago: bad decisions about hiring made by leaders and firms are not necessarily reasons to not invest in those firms; leaders and firms who live with those bad decisions *is*.

If an organization already has a significant group of "best," the leaders do not need to be very involved with the hiring of every additional member of the team, but they still have everything to do with their being let go. Too often, though, we compound our initial mistake of hiring that individual with thinking that we can change everyone. We can't. Leaders and organizations should develop team members, but their job is not to fundamentally change them. As leaders, if we allow people who don't embody our culture to continue to be a part of it, eventually the teammates who do embody it will leave our organization. Bill Gates famously said, "Don't ever hire B-level people. You will hire C-level people. And if you hire C-level people, A-level people leave." We (respectfully) disagree. A-level people don't leave your organization if you *hire* B- or C-level people. They leave if you allow them to remain.

Is this hiring process too harsh? Might this cause us to make mistakes and lose a "best" candidate during it? Admittedly, yes. However, as The Program's client and good friend Hall of Famer Carol Hutchins, Michigan's softball coach, has taught us, "If I lose a recruit, maybe she beats me twice a year. If I make a mistake on one, she beats me every day."

6

Talent Still Matters

As DISCUSSED, THE foundation of a world-class championship culture is its "best" people, those who are defined by the organization's Core Values: values that are representative of what it means to be "us" at the organization. The founder or CEO determines them. The organization's leadership team defines them. The people who embody them, though, are not necessarily "best" for our organization unless they are also very talented in the role for which we are hiring. Core Values are vital to an organization's culture and long-term success, but so is talent.

Without talent, we simply are not going to be able to compete, let alone win, on any battlefield. We may have wonderful people who embody our culture fully, but without talent, our chances of winning consistently are still going to be near zero. Thankfully, for those of us living in America—one of the most affluent nations in the world (the U.S. represents 4.5% of the global population, but 30% of the world's total GDP)—there is a wealth of talent on every battlefield. Many of us fortunate enough to be born and raised in America have an almost unlimited choice of educational opportunities as well as cultural, spiritual, and athletic activities. We live in a society that provides us with numerous opportunities to develop our natural talents and passions, and to do so from a very early age.

As one example, the Amateur Athletic Union (AAU), an organization dedicated to the promotion and development of amateur sports, has an annual revenue greater than $20 million, with membership that includes 681 girls' volleyball teams and more than 3,500 boys' basketball teams.[1] Our colleges and universities are ranked second out of eighty nations. In the past five Olympics, the United States has won 119 gold medals. China, our next closest rival, has won 73.[2] Our total medal count during that time is 2,827. All the countries of Western Europe combined have five hundred fewer.[3]

If you want to do well in life, talent really helps. Thankfully, we have an abundance of it. There are numerous ways to determine talent and most organizations have figured this out.

Every school says it's looking for "well-rounded" individuals with multiple interests. Program Founder Eric Kapitulik highlights that his classmates at the University of Chicago Booth School of Business (ranked the number one business school, according to U.S. News & World Report) were indeed extremely accomplished and interesting individuals. They also happen to have average college GPAs of 3.6 and GMAT scores of 726 (780 is a perfect score).

Harvard is one of the best universities in the world by almost any standard. It has an acceptance rate of 5.2% (out of every 100 applicants, 5.2 are admitted). The Program has worked with hundreds of Harvard's student-athletes. Our first client was the Harvard men's lacrosse team. Their head coach, John Tillman, now head coach at the University of Maryland, hired Eric to help make his team "better." The men and women with whom we have had the privilege to work, or simply interact, while on campus are truly impressive in so many facets of their lives. They also have an average high school GPA of 4.1. A 1460 SAT score at Harvard is "below average."[4]

---

[1] Information provided by the AAU home office.
[2] https://en.wikipedia.org/wiki/All-time_Olympic_Games_medal_table.
[3] Ibid.
[4] U.S. News & World Report, September 12, 2017.

The venerable investment bank, Goldman Sachs, hires 4% of all applicants. Average starting salary for an entry-level analyst is $71,000.[5] Goldman Sachs picks undergraduates most heavily from New York University and from the Ivy League schools Harvard, Columbia, and the University of Pennsylvania.[6]

Google employs more than 55,000 people, but only hires 4,000 people a year, out of a pool of 2.5 to 3.5 million applicants. At Google, Facebook, and Apple, Stanford and U.C. Berkeley rank numbers one and two for undergrad alums.[7]

Alabama Football, arguably the greatest college football dynasty in history, had the number one recruiting class in 2015, 2016, and 2017. In those years, they won the national championship twice and finished second once. The Program has never worked with Alabama Football, but we know numerous coaches on its staff. We appreciate that their excellence, as with Goldman Sachs, Google, Facebook, and Apple, is based on much more than just talent (including the greatest college football coach of all time), but regardless of the battlefield, talent matters.

Ask a group of five college coaches to rank the talent level of the players on the court in the high school basketball game they are watching, and in less than a few minutes they can. Schools, businesses, and the coaches watching the game all do a very accurate job of figuring out if certain individuals have the required talent to compete on their respective battlefields. However, most do a very poor job of determining if that talented individual *should*. "Most talented" does not necessarily mean "best"; talent combined with their team's Core Values does.

---

[5] Glassdoor, February 8, 2019.

[6] Beecher Tuttle, https://news.efinancialcareers.com/us-en/240377/the-best-universities-for-getting-a-job-at-goldman-sachs-in-the-u-s-europe-and-asia-within-ma-trading-risk-and-ops, November 13, 2018.

[7] Oliver Staley, https://qz.com/967985/silicon-valley-companies-like-apple-aapl-hires-the-most-alumni-of-these-10-universities-and-none-of-them-are-in-the-ivy-league/, April 25, 2017.

Action Items on "Best People"

1. As the leader, determine your own Core Values.
2. Ask your leadership team to help you define them for the organization.
3. Recruit people who embody your organization's Core Values. Ask your current "best" people to help you determine who they are during the hiring process.
4. As the leader, communicate immediately and often that if they embody the Core Values, your organization will be a wonderful place to work. If they don't, it will not be.
5. As the leaders, we must always remember that our time is an investment. How are we investing it? Prioritize those people who not only could give us the highest return on our investment, but on those who actually do!

Saved Round on "Best People": What about Diversity!?

If only three or four Core Values define our "best" people, doesn't this disallow any sort of diversity? The answer is yes—and no. Bad teams have lots of diversity in Core Values. Great teams have individuals who share the same Core Values, but great diversity in terms of race, sex, and socioeconomic background. A white male who grew up on a farm in New England, a black female who grew up in a city in the South, and the transgender son of Mexican immigrants can all be selfless, tough, and disciplined. They can all share the same Core Values while also bringing great diversity to a team or organization. We must never confuse values with personality, beliefs, race, or sexual orientation.

Eric Kapitulik is the white male from New England. He grew up in a middle-class family on a farm, with a dad who is a policeman and a mom who is a school teacher. He graduated from a military college and served eight years in the Marine Corps. He is a sum of those experiences. His Core Values—and hence, those of

The Program—are Selfless, Tough, and Disciplined. As Eric discusses openly, he is also a huge supporter of gay marriage and the legalization of marijuana, and would be considered liberal on virtually all social issues. You get hired and fired from The Program for being (or not being) Selfless, Tough, and Disciplined, not for being black, Hispanic, white, rich, poor, male, female, Christian, Jewish, Muslim, gay, straight, or transgender.

Diversity makes every organization better, regardless of the battlefield. It is a combat multiplier. Diversity, that is, in sex, race, socioeconomic background, sexual orientation, and religion—not in Core Values.

7

Determining Goals

We FIRST MUST determine and define our Core Values. We then must ensure that we do everything possible as leaders to hire talented people who share those Core Values.

Next, we must recognize that we all perform best within a structure. Goals and standards provide this, and we need both. Goals are *performance-based* (e.g., summiting a mountain, making a certain revenue number for the quarter, achieving a particular G.P.A., or winning the turnover battle). Failure to achieve a goal merely results in an opportunity to reattack that objective tomorrow.

Countless books have been written about goals and how to determine what they should be. George Doran's S.M.A.R.T. system for determining them has been in existence since 1981 and continues to make sense, regardless of the battlefield. Goals should be Specific, Measurable, Attainable, Relevant, and Timely. In helping us to achieve our S.M.A.R.T. goals, The Program believes that, as with Core Values, the fewer, the better. If we can't remember what our goals are, how important are they?

Second, write goals down, hang them in a prominent place, and tell everyone about them. If we don't have the conviction to do this, chances are slim that we will ever achieve them. Peer pressure is not always a bad thing. Those with great personal accountability and discipline may not need to tell others their goals in order to achieve them, but many of us don't possess these attributes.

Third, ensure that short-term goals are in alignment with long-term ones. Anything that we do now should help with what we want to accomplish in the future. If we are consistently accomplishing our short-term goals, but it does not lead to the achievement of our long-term ones, we must change them. For example, if our consistently achieving a short-term goal of fifty cold calls per day is not leading to our consistently achieving our long-term goal of $1,000,000 in sales, we must either increase the number of cold calls or change our short-term goal to, say, ten great prospect conversations. Goals, unlike our Core Values, can and should change.

Fourth, we must hold ourselves and the team accountable to achieving them. If we aren't achieving our goals, figure out why not and reattack them. If we are achieving them, celebrate them, set higher ones, and attack those.

Finally, standards reinforce our Core Values. They are the daily behaviors that we hold ourselves and our teammates accountable to meeting while accomplishing our goals. Standards and goals share a symbiotic relationship. For any single season or fiscal year, we might not meet our standards, or embody our Core Values, but still accomplish our goals. This typically occurs when we have a very talented team whom we don't necessarily "like," or even enjoy spending time with, even though in the short term we are "winning."

A strong culture, defined by our Core Values that all members of the team embody, and reinforced by standards that we consistently meet, allows us to consistently meet our goals, not just in the short term, but every term. Doing so then invariably increases the size of the talent pool of individuals who want to be part of our organization—everyone wants to be with a winner. Achieving our goals gives us an even greater opportunity to recruit and hire even more talented individuals who also already share our Core Values. Ensure that they do so.

Action Items on Goals

"What are you going to do with your life? What do you want to accomplish?" We are commonly asked this by our own parents and have asked our own children. It's an unfair question.

- Millennials will change jobs an average of four times in their first decade out of college.
- Their parents, the Gen Xers, did so twice during their first ten years out of college.
- Their grandparents held 11.7 jobs between the ages of 18 and 48 and about 27 percent of those held 15 jobs or more![1]

Figuring out what we want to be successful doing may be as difficult as being successful doing it! However, not knowing what we want to accomplish in our life should not be an excuse for accomplishing nothing this week.

1. Use S.M.A.R.T. to help figure out appropriate goals: Specific, Measurable, Attainable, Relevant, and Timely.
2. Greater duration is better, but a week is longer than most people will ever plan!
3. Plan backward from your longest duration. If my goal is to save $1,000 this year, I must have saved $500 six months from now and $250 three months from now. To achieve this, I must save approximately $20 every week. and approximately $3 every day.
4. Be aware of long-term goals, but stay focused on daily ones. They add up! In this case, my goal is to save $1,000 this year. I am aware of this, but I stay focused on saving $3 every day.
5. Goals are performance based. They reinforce what we want to achieve. If we fail, we reattack it the next day. If I don't save $3 today, I don't dwell on it; I reattack it tomorrow.

---

[1] Jeffrey R. Young, How Many Times Will People Change Jobs? The Myth of the Endlessly-Job-Hopping Millennial, https://www.edsurge.com, July 20, 2017.

Saved Round on Goals: When Do I Change Goals?

"I/we set a goal that I/we thought was going to be challenging, but attainable. As it turns out, we are going to crush it. Should I change it?"

Or

"I/we set a goal that I/we thought was going to be challenging, but attainable. As it turns out, we are going to get crushed by it. Should I change it?"

The answer is yes in either case, but the timing of when to do so is very different. In the first scenario, a leader can and should change the goal, but only after first recognizing the accomplishment of achieving what the team originally set out to do. You can change the goal prior to achieving it, but recognize its accomplishment when it is reached even if a new goal has already been set. If not, the attitude of "nothing is ever good enough" will quickly set in, which can lead to burnout and the "best" people leaving the team.

None of us like to fail in attaining our goals. However, if we are always achieving our goals, we should be setting higher ones. If we are setting S.M.A.R.T. goals, though, we will fall short occasionally and when we do, we figure out why we failed as a team, communicate those reasons, reset, and continue to attack it. A common refrain, and worry, shared by both coaches and business leaders is that if they set goals too high and their team is at a point in the season or fiscal year when they know they aren't going to reach them, then the team or certain individuals might quit. If this is the case with your team, then get rid of the team or those certain individuals on the team as quickly as possible. As a leader, there is nothing you can do about quitters except get rid of them. They are a cancer and will affect the rest of your organization if they have the influence to do so. Someone who stops trying when faced with adversity, when things don't "go their way," is the definition of a bad teammate, regardless of talent.

8

When You Face a Hairpin Turn in the Road

Cory ross—corporate president of The Program, then a Marine Corps Captain—and his teammates left the village nestled in the Tora Bora Mountains in eastern Afghanistan shortly after lunch with village elders. It was quiet and peaceful, until they reached a sharp hairpin turn in the road a few miles out of town.

A massive barrage of enemy small arms and shoulder-fired weapons assaulted them. The sound was deafening and dust filled the air as machine gun rounds impacted the dirt road, showering them with sparks flying off the vehicles' armor.

Sergeant Aaron Wittman, the vehicle's .50 caliber machine gunner, saw where the enemy fire was coming from and immediately swiveled his machine gun to return fire at the enemy position located in a nearby cemetery. When firing a vehicle-mounted machine gun, you have two options: lower yourself into the vehicle and reach up and fire the weapon one-handed, or stand tall and get in a tight position behind the weapon. You can provide much more accurate fire this way, but it exposes you to the return fire from the enemy. Sergeant Wittman chose the second option. He stood tall and fired one

28

Figure 8.1 The armored vehicle Captain Ross, Sergeant Wittman, and the rest of the team were riding in when it was hit by an RPG in Afghanistan.

long, sustained burst that alerted all his teammates to the location of the enemy position. However, in doing so, he exposed himself to the enemy and could not dodge the return fire.

An RPG is an area-fire weapon. You shoot it at an area where you want it to explode. Cory, Sergeant Wittman, and the rest of their team riding in that vehicle, had the misfortune of taking a direct hit from an RPG (see Figure 8.1). The enemy RPG passed through Sergeant Wittman and exploded inside the vehicle. Incredibly, he did not die instantly, but instead desperately clung to life.

Everyone else in the vehicle received massive injuries and most were immediately knocked unconscious. Thankfully, the driver was not. Assailed by the RPG's shrapnel, the driver, Private First Class (PFC) Potter, wasn't knocked unconscious, but a 4-inch piece of metal shot through his shoulder and was sticking out of it. Instead of attending to his own massive wound, PFC Potter moved the vehicle out of the kill zone and into a better position from which his teammates could engage the enemy, saving all their lives in the process.

The Green Beret team sergeant was severely wounded with numerous injuries, yet still coordinated his own medical evacuation (medevac) so as not to take away manpower or resources from the firepower now being used to engage with the enemy. He dragged his torn and bleeding body onto a stretcher, ensuring that the maximum number of his own teammates could stay focused on overcoming the ambush.

The Afghan interpreter, riding in the back seat of the vehicle, was flung from the vehicle and lay crumpled on the road. Initially knocked unconscious, he awoke on the side of the road with a piece of shrapnel protruding from his leg. He tied a bandanna around the wound to staunch the bleeding, grabbed his AK-47, and sprinted to the closest building to clear it of the enemy and set up a point where the team could care for their casualties.

Sergeant First Class Shaun Harris was severely concussed by the initial blast and knocked unconscious. Upon awakening, although severely concussed, he immediately started taking vital signs and giving first aid to Sergeant Wittman, who despite the aid ultimately succumbed to his wounds. Staying focused on the mission, Shaun then exited the safety of the vehicle, got behind another machine gun, and commenced firing into the enemy's position.

The Green Beret team medic, Staff Sergeant Bobby Lane, who was riding in a different vehicle, sprinted over 200 yards through intense enemy fire so that he could provide aid to his injured teammates spread throughout the convoy. He then quickly prioritized the wounded and mortally wounded while ascertaining the remaining casualties and requesting the medevac helicopter.

Cory and Army Staff Sergeant Aaron Powell were standing behind their weapon systems in the back of the M-ATV truck when the RPG hit the vehicle. Both were thrown to the floor of it and knocked unconscious by the blast. Cory awoke to the sounds of gunfire and his teammates' voices coming over the radio. This was a decision point: lie on the floor of the armored truck and survive for another few minutes, or get up and fight back? The voices of Cory's teammates on the radio reporting the casualties and the enemy's location, and the fact that they were already fighting back, made his decision easy.

However, Cory's teammate lay on top of him, unmoving, pinning Cory to the truck bed. Assuming he was dead, Cory struggled to lift his teammate off him. Cory knew more enemy rounds were inbound, but with all his gear and armor on, Staff Sergeant Powell weighed nearly 280 pounds and Cory strained to budge him. As Cory pushed against him, he heard his teammate groan and cry out in pain, indicating that he was still alive. Cory knew that Staff Sergeant Powell's .50 caliber machine gun needed to be back in the fight. Regardless of his injuries, in order for the team to survive, Staff Sergeant Powell had to return fire.

Cory positioned Staff Sergeant Powell behind the machine gun in the back of the vehicle, directed his teammate onto the enemy position, and told him to start shooting. SSG Powell continuously returned fire against the enemy force and was instrumental in suppressing the enemy, while the medevac helicopter continued to evac the wounded and deceased. Cory then lifted his own personal weapon and began firing into the cemetery as well.

Cory and his teammates fought for the next two hours. They were able to secure a nearby area from which they could call in a helicopter and evacuate their wounded. In addition, they called in several airstrikes that killed many of the enemy ambushers as they tried to escape into the mountains.

Despite the vehicle being bloody and disabled, and most of the crew severely wounded, the team drove the vehicle for an additional two hours back to their forward operating base while maintaining security through enemy-controlled territory. Later, Cory and his teammates realized that Staff Sergeant Powell had initially cried out in pain because he was severely concussed, his jaw was swollen shut, and he had broken his back in two places. Staff Sergeant Powell stayed with his teammates and was only evacuated once the convoy returned to friendly lines.

When we face an obstacle, an unexpected challenge, or a hairpin turn in the road of life, we must keep going. We must not turn back or give up, but pull ourselves and our teammates together, assess the situation, and continue to fight. We must still accomplish the mission. "Best" people consistently achieving both goals and standards help to ensure this.

When we face an obstacle, an unexpected challenge, or a hairpin turn in the road of life, we must keep going. Don't turn back. Don't give up.

9

Determining Standards

PARENTS, TEACHERS, COACHES, and business leaders all have goals for their children, students, athletes, and employees, respectively. Championship-caliber families, schools, athletic teams, and business organizations also have standards.

A "standard" is a set level of acceptable behavior that reinforces an organization's Core Values. Goals are performance based. They reinforce what we want to achieve. Failure to meet it means reattacking it tomorrow. Standards are behavior based. They reinforce who we are (our Core Values). Failure to meet a standard carries a consequence.

Some teams don't perform well because they don't have the talent to compete. That isn't "underperforming." Underperforming is when a team performs at a level below what their talent should allow them. In these cases, it is almost always due to poor culture. A culture's foundation is its Core Values, which define what it means to be a member of that team. Those values are the behaviors that every member of the team is expected to embody, but a t-shirt or a lobby poster reading "Discipline" does not make that team disciplined. An adherence to standards that reinforce Discipline does.

Once we determine our Core Values and how we define them within our organization, we must then figure out the standards needed to reinforce them daily. It is easy to *say* that our culture is based on the Core Values of honesty, commitment, and passion, but are we proving it every day? Adhering to our standards does!

For example, at The Program, our Core Values are Selflessness, Toughness, and Discipline. It would be easy for us to print "Discipline" on our t-shirts, but this doesn't make us disciplined. Instead, our standard to reinforce Discipline is that we respond to all internal or external communication (emails, voice mails, text messages, etc.) within 24 hours. For The Program team, adhering to that standard does reinforce our Core Value of Discipline!

Standards are easily understood, defined, and actionable. They are not open for interpretation. Did you or didn't you? When working with clients, The Program helps guide the "best" people as they determine their standards. We will task the "best" with creating a standard that reinforces their Core Value of Commitment. Typically, their initial attempt will be: "We will be prepared and on time for every meeting." This is good, but not great. We push back on it. It is easily understood, defined, and actionable. Unfortunately, it is very much open for interpretation. What some people consider "prepared and on time" is not necessarily what others consider it. Does it mean sitting in our seats five minutes early with a notebook and pen, or does it mean sliding in and sitting in our seats ten seconds before the start of the meeting?

"We are sitting in our seats with a notebook and pen five minutes before the start of any meeting." This is also easily understood, defined, and actionable. It is also not open for interpretation. It allows for greater team accountability because it is now no longer a personal judgment call. "Prepared" to one person may not be "prepared" for someone else, but five minutes early with a notebook and pen is the same for everyone.

Goals are performance based. They reinforce what we want to do. Standards are behavior based. They reinforce how we are expected to behave. Almost every family, school, athletic team, and corporation has goals. World-class families, schools, athletic teams, and corporations have both goals *and standards*.

Action Items on Determining Standards

1. Leader determines Core Values.
2. Leader and their closest advisors define those Core Values.
3. "Best" people determine standards that reinforce those Core Values daily (more on this in the next chapter).
4. One standard reinforces each Core Value (i.e., three Core Values, three or four Standards).
5. Once a standard has become an *expectation*, raise the standard.

Saved Round on Determining Standards

Kids these days. What do PFC Potter, Sergeant Aaron Wittman, Staff Sergeant Powell, and Staff Sergeant Bobby Lane have in common? They are all part of the millennial generation, one of the "kids these days," and they all saved the life of someone who was not. They are just one example of why you will never hear any member of The Program team talk about the "kids these days."

We believe that we live in the greatest country on Earth. We hope everyone feels this way about their own country. We know that our elected officials make mistakes, but we are so thankful that we have had the privilege to live in and serve this country. We do, however, feel that several challenges are facing our society. One of the biggest mistakes we see occurring in our society is a lack of standards and then a commitment to them. Starting in the homes that our young people grow up in and then in the schools they attend, the athletic teams they play for, and the companies where they work, there are a lot of goals but never any standards, or if there are, there is no commitment to them.

We all perform best with structure in our life. Not military left-foot, right-foot structure, but an understanding of what we are expected to achieve and how we are expected to *behave*. As discussed earlier, goals are performance based. They help outline what we want to accomplish. Standards, in contrast, are behavior based. They outline how we behave. Fail to reach a goal, reattack it tomorrow. Fail to reach a standard, however, and there are consequences.

All of us perform best with structure. Goals and standards provide it.

Almost every leader claims to have high standards, but if there is no consequence when a member of the team fails to achieve them, by definition, there are no standards. This has become ubiquitous throughout our society: pop positive on a drug test, don't worry—everyone is doing it. Get caught cheating or get a bad grade, blame the teacher. Be physically or emotionally abusive to a female co-worker or classmate, be suspended from the team for just the first half of a game, probably against a team whom we'll beat by thirty anyway.

The "kids these days," are no different from any other generation before them. Stop blaming them for their deficiencies, perceived or actual. They grow up in homes, live in communities, attend schools, compete on athletic teams, and work at organizations that lack standards, that lack consequences. Everything is a goal. That isn't the fault of the "kids these days." That is our fault as parents, teachers, coaches, and business leaders. Our job as leaders is to provide structure within which our young people can develop. We have failed to do so. We have provided this younger generation with lots of goals (what we expect them to *achieve*), but rarely any standards (how we expect them to *behave*).

We must provide both.

10

A Commitment to Goals and Standards

WE HAVE SEEN numerous examples of a great parent, coach, or business leader *creating* a world-class championship culture through sheer force of will. They refuse to accept mediocrity and single-handedly carry the entire organization to the mountaintop. It is incredibly physically, mentally, and emotionally challenging to bring the team there, but a physically, mentally, and emotionally tough leader can do it (more on developing these attributes in Section 4).

However, *sustaining* a world-class championship culture over the long term takes a commitment from the entire team. World-class organizations have world-class cultures whose foundation is its "best" people. We then must provide structure to those "best" people where they can develop and then perform at their best. That structure is defined by our goals and standards. Finally, world-class organizations are committed to achieving those goals and standards. The leader is not the only one committed. Although we can *do it* alone, we cannot *sustain it* alone; it requires the entire organization. To create this commitment, we must give ownership to our "best" people, those team members who have talent and embody our organization's Core Values.

We consistently hear coaches and business leaders agree that to be successful or to become even more successful, the team must be more committed. They correctly surmise that providing "ownership" of the team to the members of it helps them be more committed. Leaders typically attempt to accomplish this by allowing team members to decide where they want to eat while on the road. Unfortunately, this does not give them ownership; it merely makes them food critics!

To create ownership, we must first identify our Core Values, explain how we define them for our organization, and then identify those individuals who best embody them. At that point, we can task our "best" people with creating the goals and standards that reinforce those Core Values. These are the goals and standards to which they first want to be held. Second are the goals and standards to which they will hold each other, and finally those to which they want to hold their teammates accountable. We allow and foster ownership by selecting and tasking those players or employees whom we view as "best" to determine our organization's goals and standards. All of us love ownership, especially the "best" people. Give it to them! If our best people, and then the team, *own* the goals and standards, they own the team's culture.

The "best" people appreciate the trust we put in them to determine what the goals and standards should be. They are more committed to enforcing and reinforcing them because these are the goals and standards that they said *they* wanted! They are their goals and standards.

Leaders often question this approach. What if the best people set goals and standards that are too low? We appreciate the concern.

However, numerous clients who tried this approach have reported back to us that not only did their "best" not set too low of goals and standards, but rather provided ones that were unrealistically high for anyone on the team other than the "best." The leaders had to introduce a bit of "reasonable person theory" into the discussion about what the team's goals and standards should be. Leaders do this by making goals and standards more "gateway," meaning slightly lower standards at the start that act as *gateways* to higher ones in the future. Our "best" people don't want to associate with anything, or anyone, who is also not the best. Lions hang out with lions, zebras with zebras.

We ensure an unprecedented commitment level to our organization and the goals and standards that reinforce our culture, our Core Values, by giving true ownership of the team to the team's "best" people. We do so by allowing our "best" to determine the goals and, more importantly, the standards to which they will hold themselves first and then their teammates (including the leaders).

11

Hold "Best" Accountable

LEADERS CAN CREATE a world-class championship culture, but it takes others to sustain it. In keeping with the approach of allowing our "best" to determine the goals and, more importantly, the standards of our organization, if standards are not met, the leader should not be the one to correct those failing to meet them. Instead, the leader holds the "best" people accountable for doing so. Remember, it is their own standards that are not being met, the ones to which they said they wanted to be held accountable and to which they would hold the team. The "best" *own* the standards. If their standards are not being met by any person in the organization, it is the responsibility of the "best" people—not the head coach, warehouse supervisor, or regional sales director—to hold those individuals or the team accountable.

Too often, we task the "best" with determining the goals and standards, but instead of holding them accountable, leaders hold the whole team accountable. Hold the "best" accountable! If they don't want to be held accountable, they aren't one of the "best."

Finally, world-class championship teams have world-class championship cultures. They have both S.M.A.R.T. goals and high standards. They are committed to both. If a goal is not met, reattack it. If it is, celebrate it. Typically, this occurs naturally (i.e., a cheering crowd, greater publicity, or financial compensation). If a standard is not met, hold our "best" accountable and enforce a consequence. More importantly, we must ensure that when standards are met, there is also a benefit. Exceptional performance is always recognized. Leaders must ensure that exceptional behavior is celebrated even more.

The average American male gains two pounds of body weight every year after they graduate from college. On the morning of their twenty-year reunion, they look at themselves in the mirror and think, "I'm fat." But it didn't occur overnight; we just happened to notice it that morning. It has been happening for the past twenty years, two pounds at a time. The same happens to our culture. Specifically, our standards are lowered two pounds at a time until eventually our cultures are no longer world-class. Leaders work tirelessly to create a championship culture, but it takes a team to sustain it.

As Marine Corps drill instructors know, "The standard you walk past is the new standard that you set." All of us, at times, become tired and frustrated. We have challenging weeks and months. Eventually, we see a standard not being met and we walk past "it." Unfortunately, *it* becomes the new standard, a lower standard. We "gain two pounds." Don't allow it. Providing ownership to our "best" people, by allowing them to determine our organization's standards and holding them accountable when they are not met, as well as when they are, ensures that we have a team of committed individuals. It ensures that we don't wake up one morning and dislike our team's culture as much as we dislike the reflection we see in the mirror on the morning of our twenty-year reunion.

Action Items on a Commitment to Goals and Standards

1. "Best" people are the foundation of a world-class championship culture. Task them with determining our organization's goals and standards.
2. Standards:
   a. Reinforce our organization's Core Values.
   b. Address the "Mission Critical" areas of our team that must be addressed right now!
   c. Are the behaviors they want to hold themselves and their teammates accountable to achieving.

3. "Gateway" standards: Generally, Core Values don't change. Standards can. Pick appropriate standards that reinforce the behaviors we need our team to achieve now, standards that will act as a "gateway" to higher ones in the future.
4. If standards are not met, leaders hold the "best" people accountable and ensure there is a consequence.
5. If standards are met, leaders hold the "best" people accountable and provide a benefit.
6. Be transparent. Communicate, communicate, communicate our Core Values, our standards, and both the consequences for failing to meet them and the benefits for doing so.

Saved Rounds on a Commitment to Goals and Standards

Complacency kills, on any battlefield. We win five games in a row and individuals on the team become complacent. The same is true when we retain the number one position in our industry. Coaches and business leaders are aware of this and constantly stress the importance and the need for the team to continue to practice and perform consistently as required by our goals. No leader gets that excited about the "score" after one or two quarters on any battlefield. Despite the current "score," leaders stay focused on their long-term goals and ensure their teams do as well.

Unfortunately, we forget to reinforce our standards. After a great start to the season or exceeding sales goals in the first quarter, leaders often tell us that their teams "got it."

As leaders, as soon as we feel this way, we must clearly communicate our team's standards. When our teams say they know the standards, communicate them again—before, during, and after practice; before, during, and after every game; before, during, and after every weekly, quarterly, and annual meeting. Knowing that complacency can occur, leaders consistently reinforce their expectations of how we are supposed to perform or continue to

(continued)

Saved Rounds on a Commitment to Goals and Standards (Cont'd)

perform, and do so even more after a five-game winning streak or a quick start to the fiscal year. We must recognize that complacency occurs within our culture as well.

Goals reinforce what we want to achieve. Knowing them is important. Standards reinforce how we need to behave to achieve those goals. Both are vital to our success. Leaders must be sure that their team is aware of the goal. This is almost always the case, though: no one forgets that they are trying to win a championship or finish first in their industry. More importantly, leaders must ensure their team stays focused on their standards and their behaviors every single day as they fight to attain that goal. Leaders do so by continuously communicating, enforcing, and recognizing standards.

Team members will get complacent. We can survive this. When leaders get complacent, we die.

SECTION

II

Teammates

JAMEY LISTENED AS the countdown came over the radio. "5, 4, 3, 2..." No targets presented themselves, so the snipers held their fire and the night stayed quiet. Jamey tightened as the "1" sounded, bracing himself for the explosion and then to storm through the door. When the thunderously loud blast came, Jamey and his teammates were thrown to the ground and the night air was filled with smoke, coughs, and screams.

Master Sergeant Glenn Cederholm (left) and Master Sergeant James Slife (right) in Baghdad, Iraq.

Note: Photo courtesy of Master Sergeant James Slife.

12

A Special Operations Teammate

ON JUNE 19, 2003, Marine Corps Special Operations Detachment One (Det 1) was activated. The Program Director of Operations, Jamey Slife, then a Staff Sergeant, was one of its founding members. Jamey and his teammates at Det 1 were hand-selected from thousands of possible candidates. They were assessed on intelligence, physical and mental toughness, tactical and technical proficiency, and personal character. Colonel Robert Coates, Det 1's Commanding Officer, wanted "tough, rugged bastards." Jamey was further selected to be part of the forty-man assault force. Their primary mission was direct-action operations against high-value enemy targets.

Det 1 had seven months to train before deploying to Iraq. It was brutally intense. Every Thursday morning, they would hike at least 15 miles with a 50-pound rucksack (backpack). At the conclusion of the hike, they would engage in various physical team competitions. Their "workday" would begin upon completion. Each sailor and Marine conservatively shot one hundred thousand rounds of ammunition from both their M4 carbine long rifles and Kimber .45 caliber special operations handguns. They would freefall-jump out of airplanes at twenty-five thousand feet in the dark of night with 50–75 pounds of combat equipment strapped to them. They would dive out of submarines and then kick-fin while pushing their packs and weapons in front of them over 5 miles to land. They would spend weeks in the forest or desert living only off what they could carry or forage.

They pushed themselves past the point of physical and mental failure, which was not only condoned, but expected. They learned from each failure, becoming smarter, stronger, faster, tougher, and more proficient.

We all fill one of two roles in our families, athletic teams, school groups, or corporations: either teammate or team leader. For any organization to be successful, we must have great leadership (more on this in the following section). However, not every member of our team or organization is a leader, nor do we need them to be. We don't need all forty Marines of the Det 1 Assault Force to be leaders, nor a hundred leaders on a football team, fifteen leaders on a basketball team, nor a thousand leaders in a manufacturing company. Sometimes Mom is in charge and sometimes Dad.

Some of the toughest, most courageous, dependable, and honorable men and women with whom we have had the pleasure of serving with weren't leaders. They were outstanding teammates and our teams could never have accomplished our missions, much less survived, without them. This is true for every team. Not every person on a team is a leader, but simply by being a member of it, we are all teammates.

Teammates are held to two standards: meet the organization's standards and then hold teammates accountable to meeting them. Great teammates consistently achieve both.

The quality of the Marines selected for Det 1, their development throughout an incredibly intense training period prior to deployment, and then an extreme focus on detailed planning for combat operations while in Iraq, helped ensure their success. Det 1 conducted hundreds of missions that went "according to plan," or at the very least, without a major incident. One did not....

13

Meet the Standards: Be a Thumb Teammate!

JAM YOUR THUMB into your chest repeatedly. That is being a *thumb teammate*. Point your index finger at a teammate. That is being a *finger* teammate.

Great teammates consistently meet the organization's standards, and then hold their teammates accountable to achieving them. Accountability makes us the best versions of ourselves. Our competition, and the battlefields where we compete, will demand our very best. Unfortunately, if we wait until those moments to give it, we are doomed to mission failure. Great teammates understand this. Great teammates hold teammates accountable, but to do so successfully, we must first be "a thumb teammate." As discussed in Chapter 2, one of the first lessons all Marine Corps officers are taught is "Never ask a Marine to do something that you aren't willing to do yourself." Otherwise, Marines will never trust or respect you, both vital characteristics of teammates in any world-class organization, and often two of the Core Values of high-performing teams.

Too often though, teammates cut corners on Monday, but then try to hold other teammates accountable for the same issue on Tuesday. We have no right to be "a finger teammate" if we have not already been "a thumb teammate" first. An *unwillingness* to do so causes individual relationships and teams to fracture and fail. Standards reinforce behaviors and how we behave requires us to make a choice. It does not require talent. Therefore, if we choose not to be "a thumb teammate," it is due to an *unwillingness*, not an *inability*.

On the night of May 24, 2004, Det 1's mission, named Operation Ricochet, was to capture a known improvised explosive device (IED) maker. They planned on hitting his house late at night, using an explosive breach (bomb) to blow the door off the hinges and then pull him out of bed before he, or any of his associates, had time to react. They had trained and successfully executed similar missions multiple times without major incident. This night would be different.

The Assault Force had been broken down into six smaller six- or seven-man teams. On previous missions, Teams 1 and 3 had proven themselves and been very successful as the "main effort," the teams placing the breach and removing the bad guy from the crisis site. During Operation Ricochet, Det 1 leaders had decided to switch the teams.

A breacher is the individual in the assaulting force responsible for making the explosive charge that will be placed on a door or wall on the objective site. He is then responsible for exploding that charge. The explosion would blow the door off the hinges and into the room. The assaulters would immediately "ride" the breach into the crisis site. They would use the resulting noise, smoke, confusion, and chaos of the explosion to capture or kill any enemies before they had time to react.

All members of Det 1 were extremely talented at their chosen profession. They didn't just have Marines with sniper qualifications; they had the best snipers in the Marine Corps. The same was true for their radiomen, explosive experts (breachers), corpsmen, and every other role in Det 1, including their support personnel. Every member was extremely talented, but also tough, selfless, competitive, and disciplined.

Det 1 had chosen to use a certain type of explosive breach while conducting these operations due to the chaos and confusion it caused the enemy. If done properly, the enemy would have no time to respond before the assault force was in the objective area and gaining fire superiority. Almost instantaneous with the breach exploding, Det 1 Marines would be "on top of" the bad guys.

All the breachers were trained to the same standard. There were standards for the type of explosive charge to be used and how it was to be placed on the door. Understanding that the enemy, the battlefield, and other factors might make them deviate from the standard, there was a standard that any changes be communicated to everyone on the team. There was also a standard that the more experienced breachers check the new, less experienced breachers' explosive charges. There were numerous other standards as well. Unfortunately, it was these that would come back to haunt the assault force in the early morning hours of May 24, 2004.

In the short term, enough talent can compensate for standards not being met on any battlefield. Talent *can* "win games." However, choosing not to meet standards will eventually catch up to anyone and every team, regardless of talent level. In contrast, talent combined with our choosing to consistently meet the standards, to be a thumb teammate first, allows us to consistently accomplish the mission regardless of our chosen battlefield.

Make a commitment to be a thumb teammate first. If we *behave* at a world-class level consistently, we will *perform* at a world class level just as consistently. It doesn't guarantee mission accomplishment or winning a championship, but first meeting the standard, and then ensuring everyone else does as well, ensures that we will have the opportunity to compete for them. A "thumb teammate" is synonymous with the first standard of being a great teammate (meet the standards of your team) and is vital to successfully accomplishing the second (holding our teammates accountable to meeting them).

14

Do Your Job! Agreed, Kinda...

"DOING YOUR JOB" is defined by most athletes, teachers, coaches, and business leaders as accomplishing the necessary tasks associated with their title on the team. Most even define themselves by it: when asked, "What do you do?" they respond with their title: "I am a football player" or more specifically, "I am a wide receiver." Or "I am a point guard," "I am a salesperson," "I am a doctor," "I am a plant manager." With this definition, most people believe that doing their "job" is synonymous with "meeting the standard." It is not!

For a team to do well, for a business to make its budget, or an athletic team to win a lot of games, the members of the team must perform the tasks associated with their title at a high level. A wide receiver must catch footballs. A point guard must dribble well and make good decisions with the basketball. A salesperson must sell the services or products for which they are responsible. An emergency room doctor must save lives, and a plant manager must ensure that the plant runs smoothly. Many leaders, wide receivers, point guards, salespeople, ER doctors, and plant managers believe that this is *their job*. It is not. This is "performing the tasks associated with your title." It is hugely important, but it is not *your job*.

To accomplish our mission, to compete for championships on any battlefield, and to do so on a consistent basis, we must expand this very narrow definition of "job." Talent and hard work allow us to do well in accomplishing the tasks associated with our title. Do this very

50

narrowly defined "job" well and those individuals will help the team win "games," on whatever our chosen playing field or battlefield. However, to consistently accomplish the mission, compete for championships, or perform at a world-class level, we must do this and never forget that we are also members of a greater team. Individuals can do well, but great teams compete for championships regardless of the field of battle.

Every member of the team must *do their job*. Our "job," however, is to be great teammates (and great team leaders). As discussed in Section 1, our best people and greatest teammates have the necessary talent to accomplish the tasks associated with their title *and* they embody our team's Core Values, our culture. They embody this culture by meeting the standards that reinforce it.

Every member of the team must do their job. Our "job" however, is to be great teammates (and great team leaders).

15

Winning Still Matters

ERIC'S SON, AXEL, attends a well-to-do private school. He came home from school one day and told Eric that he was taught that it doesn't matter if you win or lose, only if you *have fun*. Eric immediately asked Axel if he gets more enjoyment—if he has more fun—at wrestling when he is getting pinned or when he is pinning his opponent? Eric asked Axel if he really likes getting over the obstacles at the indoor obstacle course they go to or if he feels just as good when he can't get over one. Eric asked him if he is happier when he gets a gold star on his homework assignments or when it is marked in red.

Winning and losing matter. Be aware of it. Just don't focus on it. Focus instead on behaviors, on meeting team standards. Great teammates do. Standards have nothing to do with talent; they are a choice. Axel might not be able to dribble a basketball, but he can still be a *tough* basketball player if he achieves the standards that reinforce tough on his basketball team (i.e., dive for loose balls, help teammates and opponents off the floor).

> *Winning and losing matter. Be aware of it. Just don't focus on it. Focus instead on behaviors, on meeting team standards. Great teammates do.*

Remember that goals are performance based. Standards are behavior based. Goals reinforce what we want to accomplish. Standards reinforce how we behave. Axel is extremely happy when he pins his wrestling opponent, gets over an obstacle, or receives a gold star for his homework. Of course, Axel gets excited about winning and is naturally

52

disappointed when he doesn't. Further, he is seven years old, so he will spend his entire life in an age of social media.

Therefore, someday a lot of people might make a big deal if he can dribble a basketball really well. There is also the possibility that a huge number of people will make a really big deal about it if he doesn't dribble it very well in a game. Instead of worrying about people who might be happy or angry with him due to his ability to dribble, Eric hopes he stays focused on being selfless, tough, and disciplined, Team Kapitulik's Core Values. Consistent behaviors will determine Axel's (and all of our) consistent success on whatever the battlefield.

There are a thousand things that Axel doesn't control that can contribute to his dribbling a basketball well in a game. The other team may just deny him the ball. The same is true for his performance at school. He could choose to take a really easy course and get an A, or a very difficult one and get a B (or like his father, a C). The most successful individuals and teams stay focused only on what they can control, and we control our behaviors. Doing so will allow us to compete for championships on whatever our chosen battlefield.

With that said, if we had asked Jamey and his teammates if winning or losing mattered just prior to the start of Operation Ricochet, they would have thought the question rhetorical. Winning matters and great teammates help their teams win.

We must always be aware of our performance, aware of our team's goals, but we must focus on how we are to achieve them, we must focus on meeting our team's standards.

Action Items on Meeting the Standard

"Self-discipline is something—it's like a muscle. The more you exercise it, the stronger it gets."—psychologist Daniel Goldstein

1. Doing anything consistently requires discipline. There is no substitute for it. If we want to be more disciplined, exercise it today: meet the standard.
2. Trust is the foundation of every relationship. Never do anything to undermine that trust. A poor teammate may meet the standard on the field or during the workday, but then not do so on Saturday night or during a business trip when no one is

(continued)

watching. A great teammate meets the standard in all aspects of life. Doing so develops trust (and requires discipline).

3. Hitting a homerun requires something more than simply choosing to do so. It requires talent. Meeting the standard does not! Choose to do so.

Saved Round on Meeting the Standard

Take strain. We all have a different definition of success, but most of us would agree that to be successful on whatever our chosen battlefield, we will have to give great effort.

Prior to an SEC football game, Coach Butch Jones addressed his team: "Effort is the weakest word in the English language. Giving effort is the price of admission just to step on the field on this team and in the SEC. Plus, I know guys are going to give effort. I want to see who will take strain *from* their teammates. I want to see who will sacrifice and put more on his own shoulders to help his teammates and this team."

Giving great effort benefits the team, but it also benefits the person who is giving it. There is nothing wrong at all with this fact, but it is a fact. People who give great effort do help the team, but they also help themselves in the process. However, the most successful teams have teammates who give effort and "take strain" from their teammates. They sacrifice for one another.

Effort always benefits the individual giving it. Taking strain may not, but it will make our teammates trust and respect us, and it always makes our team better.

It isn't just about what we do (effort), but rather what we are willing to sacrifice (strain) for our teammates. Are we willing to sacrifice going to a party or staying out late so that we can watch more game film? Are we willing to cover assignments for a corporate teammate who needs to leave early? Are we willing to make better decisions nutritionally and sacrifice the chips and fast food or soda that we crave so that we can lose weight and play with our kids more? Are we willing to wake up in the middle of the night, even when it isn't our "turn", to comfort a crying baby so our partner can sleep more?

Great teammates don't just give great effort. They take strain.

16

Great Teammates Hold One Another Accountable

Great teammates meet the standards and then hold their teammates accountable. Most teammates meet the standards of the organization. It requires hard work and a "care factor." Regardless of the battlefield, most teammates do give effort and they do care about the team. Holding one another accountable is extremely challenging for us all, however, and it is why there are so few great teammates and one of the main reasons why there are so few truly world class organizations. Following are the five main reasons why it is so challenging.

First, almost all of us have been taught from a very young age to "be nice." We should. It costs nothing and it's easy to be nice. Unfortunately, we aren't taught what it means to be truly "kind." Nice is saying hello, asking about a teammate's welfare, sitting with a new teammate at lunch. Being nice generally involves providing comfort. Kind is holding a teammate accountable. Kind is helping to make our teammates the best version of themselves. Even though it is incredibly uncomfortable for us to hold teammates accountable, we do so anyway because it *is* in their best interest. If you are a good person, being nice should be relatively easy. Being kind and holding our teammates accountable is not. It requires a sacrifice. Many teammates are unwilling to make that sacrifice.

55

Second, there are very few people who enjoy personal confrontation. As discussed, it makes us extremely uncomfortable. It is uncomfortable to hold anyone accountable, let alone a teammate who might be older or a higher performer than us. Anything that we do habitually is easier than those things that we must *think* about doing. Leaders must make it easier for teammates to hold each other accountable. If we are to create a culture of accountability, we must create an environment where accountability can become a habit.

Third, many of us have been told throughout our lives to "lead by example." We then see or hear our mentors consistently recognize others who are doing so. Typically, someone who *leads by example* is an individual who works extremely hard in their preparation, consistently gives 100% in all facets of their life, and when it is time to perform, they perform. They are quiet. They don't say anything to anyone else, but they prepare and perform at the highest levels. Unfortunately, our own parents, teachers, coaches, and business leaders reinforce this belief that those individuals are *leading by example* because of this. Parents, coaches and business leaders are wrong. We will explain why.

Fourth, teammates don't hold one another accountable because of a lack of trust. We don't trust our teammates who are being held accountable to respond in a positive manner or improve because of it. Leaders further undermine the team's trust by holding different teammates accountable to different standards or by failing to enforce a consequence when standards are not met. Trust is the foundation of every relationship and consistently meeting and enforcing standards builds it. Unfortunately, the opposite occurs when standards are not met or not enforced.

Finally, team cohesion is many team's greatest strength. It is also their greatest weakness. Thanks to our egos, we all have a strong desire to be well liked. We want to be good friends to everyone and for them to be good friends to us. Some teammates, due to a lack of confidence, maturity, emotional resilience, and a host of other factors, might not appreciate being held accountable; they won't appreciate being challenged to get better. Our attempting to do so might make them not want to be friends with us. Rather than risk losing a friend or being considered one, we don't hold that teammate or others accountable. We prioritize being a good friend over being a great teammate. As parents, we do so with our own children. We would rather be good friends to them rather than great teammates. The same occurs in classrooms, on athletic teams, in civic and religious organizations, and within corporations. Great team cohesion, everyone being good friends *with* each other, is a great strength for any organization, except when it comes at the price of our being great *for* each other.

The following chapters provide thoughts, suggestions and solutions to each of the previous five reasons why teammates don't hold each other accountable. First, the conclusion of Operation Richochet…

17

We Have Seen the Enemy

WE HAVE SEEN the enemy...and it is us. It is incredibly challenging to win consistently on any battlefield. Our competitors, and a host of other factors outside of our control, make it so. It is even more challenging when we do things to sabotage our own success.

During Operation Ricochet, once the decision to switch the teams responsible for the main effort occurred, a proper turnover of Teams 1 and 3's previous "actions on the objective" should have been communicated and then overcommunicated to Teams 2, 4, and 6. It was the standard. However, this standard was not met and no one said or, more importantly, did anything about it. The primary breachers from Teams 1 and 3 should have checked the oncoming breachers' explosive charges and verified that they had followed standard operating procedures. Rather than waiting for something bad to occur, before the mission ever commenced, the more experienced breachers from Teams 1 and 3 should have held their teammates accountable to the standards that were already in place. They did not.

Teammates must hold one another accountable in order to help ensure mission accomplishment. Det 1 didn't and members of their team would suffer dire consequences because of it. Although the consequences for our not doing so may be considerably different, we will suffer them just the same. Maybe not today, or next week, or even next month, but a teammate and our team will eventually pay the price.

Det 1 arrived at their objective at 0300. It was completely dark, and the buildings were quiet. Two teams moved in under the cover of darkness to set up perimeter security and ensure that no enemy was able to enter or leave the objective area. Snipers found overwatch positions and scanned the objective, searching for targets and any information about its layout that they could report back to the command element to assist the assault team. Overhead, an AC-130 Spectre gunship made lazy circles in the dark sky, ready to use its deadly arsenal of 25 mm Gatling guns, and 40 mm and 105 mm cannons.

Quickly and silently, the assault team crept in and lined up against the wall near the front door. This line of warriors is known as a "stack." Everyone in the stack has a specific role and will enter the house in a predesignated manner. It is like running an in-bounds play in basketball, a point-corner in field hockey, or any number of surgeries that occur in a hospital's emergency room. If any member of the stack makes a mistake or misses his assignment, the results can be disastrous.

With enough talent, we can all have "a good day," regardless of our preparation, or our behaviors, but over the long run, our behaviors drive our performance. *Behave* at a world-class level consistently and we will *perform* at one just as consistently. It doesn't guarantee "winning a championship," but consistently meeting the standards, and then holding our teammates accountable to them, ensures that we will consistently compete for them on whatever our chosen battlefield. The same is true if we do not.

With enough talent, we can all have "a good day," regardless of our preparation, or our behaviors, but over the long run, our behaviors drive our performance.

18

The Price of Not Holding Teammates Accountable

WHILE THE REST of the team provided security, the breacher quietly placed the explosive charge on the door and ran the wire back to the stack so he could initiate the explosion. Typically, there is a countdown on the radio: 5, 4, 3, and on the "T" of 2, snipers will shoot any target they have, ensuring that their rounds are fired simultaneously with the detonation of the explosive charge. On "1" the breacher presses the button, or "clacker", to create the explosion. Immediately, the team flows into the house, relying on speed, surprise, and violence of action to gain fire superiority on the enemy within.

Jamey was in the middle of the stack. He was there primarily as a shooter, but was also prepared to be the alternate breacher if needed. Jamey and his teammates all wore night-vision goggles that bathed everything in an ethereal green glow. They stacked tightly against the wall, silently feeding off each other's focus and adrenaline. Jamey listened as the countdown came over the radio, "5, 4, 3, 2…." No targets presented themselves so the snipers held their fire and the night stayed quiet. Jamey tightened up as the "1" sounded, bracing himself for the explosion and readying himself to storm through the door. Instead, as the charge exploded, members of the stack were blown to the ground and the night air was filled with smoke, coughs, and screams.

The breacher had used two charges instead of one. One of the charges was still attached to his gear when he hit the clacker. His bulletproof vest protected his torso from the blast, but most of his upper arm was sheared from his body. Additionally, because he had used a different adhesive than usual, the other breach had fallen off the door before it exploded. This meant that instead of the blast going into the door, it now came directly back at the tightly stacked team of Marines.

An explosive breach causes chaos and confuses the enemy. If done properly, the enemy has no time to respond before the assault team is "on top of them." However, now the chaos and confusion were on the wrong side of the door. The breacher was down and bleeding profusely. The rest of the assaulting force was in momentary disarray from the blast. This gave the enemy time to respond. The Det 1 Marines received this response in the form of AK-47 rounds exploding through the wall around them.

Because some teammates failed to meet the standard and others failed to hold them accountable, Det 1 had placed themselves in this position. There are thousands of things we don't control on the battlefields we compete on in our daily lives, but we do control meeting the standards and holding our teammates accountable to them. Det 1 hadn't, and they were fighting for their lives because of it.

19

The Benefit of Team Accountability

ON JUNE 19, 2003, Det 1 was activated. The next seven months of their lives were filled with brutally intense days of training. Fifteen-mile hikes with 50-pound rucksacks were followed by "team competitions," like rolling an 800-pound tire three miles. This was the norm *before* starting their workday. They made, placed, and exploded countless charges and entered hundreds of training crisis sites with them. Already world-class marksmen, they shot tens of thousands of rounds. Day and night, they jumped from helicopters and airplanes at every altitude. They swam from submarines miles out to sea and with the fins on their feet as their only propulsion, kicked their way onto the coastline, where they commenced multiple-week reconnaissance patrols.

These were incredibly tough men who proved it every single day throughout the seven months of their pre-deployment training. They continued to do so upon arrival in Iraq. If anything, their training only intensified. These warriors had incredibly high standards. Their commanding officer, Colonel Robert Coates, tolerated nothing less, nor did the Marines themselves. Like all great warriors, they wanted high standards and they wanted to be held to those same high standards. Yes, they were military warriors, but they were also spouses to those they loved dearly and parents to little boys and girls whom they adored. Not meeting the standard was simply not tolerated. Any "weak link" could cost other teammates their lives, and deprive families of a spouse and parent.

Performance goals started high and only increased throughout training and combat. Det 1 breachers, already experts in their field, made and exploded charges over and over again. At that point, if the breacher did not meet the goal, they did it again. And then again. Once they met the goal, the goals were raised. This was also the case for every other Marine in the unit. Every Marine had to be tough, and their training was exceedingly so. Being tough is a behavior, and so is being competitive. Behavior standards were clear, understandable, and exceedingly high for every member of the unit. Det 1 Marines had to sacrifice for one another. They had to be disciplined, competitive, and above all else, like their commanding officer, they had to be tough.

On the night of May 24, 2003, the mislaid charge's explosion tore through the Det 1 assaulting force and knocked them to the ground. The breacher, their teammate, lay bleeding profusely. A wave of AK-47 rounds crashed upon them. Even through the chaos and confusion, the Marines knew their mission, and, to accomplish it, they still needed to get inside the house. Acting quickly, Program Director of Operations, then Staff Sergeant Jamey Slife, placed another explosive charge on the door and detonated it, blowing the door inside the room.

The failed breach's explosion had disoriented many of the Det 1 Marines and caused a moment of hesitation until they regained their equilibrium. This hesitation caused another teammate to be shot as they entered the crisis site. The enemy had been given the initial momentum. Det 1 now took it back.

Standards had not been met that night, nor were teammates held accountable. Det 1 had paid the price for not doing so up to this point in the operation. Now, thanks to the thousands of standards that had been met—and thanks to the fact that individuals were held accountable when standards were not met—both during training and in this theater of combat, Det 1 had the ability to make the enemy pay from this point forward.

The first two Det 1 Marines burst through the door, trusting implicitly that their teammates would follow them. Falling back on the standards they had met, or been held accountable to meet through thousands of hours of training and combat operations, the rest of the team did follow. It was the standard. They responded to the chaos, confusion, and adversity with decisive force, overwhelming firepower, and violent action. In doing so, the house was "cleared," and an IED maker responsible for countless deaths was captured.

The level of fear, anger, chaos, and adversity felt by every member of Det 1 on that night is unfathomable for most of us. We try to put ourselves into that almost unimaginable situation and wonder how we would have responded. We never know how we will react in these life-or-death situations until we are in one ourselves, but it is easy for us as readers to label all these warriors heroes.

Yet, they will tell us that they did not behave heroically. When things were at their worst, they simply met the standards. They were able to do so not because they "rose to the occasion," but because they, like all of us, "fell back" on the habits that they had created by meeting the standards throughout thousands of hours of training and previous combat operations. If those standards were not met, individuals were held accountable and consequences were enforced—most typically, to do it again and again and again, until the standards were met. And then to do it again. If we have met the standard and held our team-mates accountable to doing the same, then when adversity strikes on our own battlefields, we will still accomplish the mission. As previously discussed, holding teammates accountable is challenging for five main reasons. The following chapters provide solutions to how we can over-come all of them.

20

Nice and Kind

Holding our teammates accountable when they fail to meet the standard makes us uncomfortable. This is as true for the best athletes in the world as it is for their coaches. It is as true for CEOs of Fortune 500 companies as it is for their corporate teammates. Despite our feeling of discomfort, we still do it for two reasons. First, we care about the success of the organization above all else. Second, we truly care about the teammates we are holding accountable. No one—at least no one we would want on our team—truly enjoys holding another accountable. Initially, it may in fact upset our teammates. No one likes to hear that they are "falling short." Therefore, many people with whom we work say that they avoid holding their teammates accountable because they "don't want to hurt their feelings." We appreciate this. We have all been taught from a very young age to "be nice."

Eric Kapitulik's son, Axel, attends a school that has a "Kindness Initiative." Teachers and coaches continuously reinforce the importance of treating classmates and all members of the school community with kindness. If someone falls, help them up. If someone is crying, ask what is wrong. If someone is sitting on the "Kindness Bench" (a bench on the playground where a child who is feeling lonely can go and sit), someone else takes it upon themselves to sit with them. Say hello. Hold the door open. Hold hands. Say please and thank you. Smile. Be kind.

Eric and his wife, Melissa, love Axel's school, his teachers, the administration, and the Kindness Initiative. It reinforces many of the things that as parents, Eric and his wife strive to teach Axel at home. Almost all parents do the same. The only difference is that Eric and The Program consider these behaviors to be random acts of niceness. Not kindness. We believe that kindness encompasses so much more.

Specifically, great teammates prove their kindness by holding their teammates accountable. It is uncomfortable to do so. Therefore, by doing so, great teammates are saying that their teammate improving and becoming the best version of themselves is more important than any feeling of discomfort that they might feel personally while holding them accountable.

Do we want to be a *nice* friend, parent, co-worker, coach, or boss who says hello to those in their spheres of influence every morning, smiles, says "please" and "thank you," and always tells everyone what a "great job" they are doing even as their playing time or end-of-year bonus diminishes? Or do we want to be a *kind* one who tells those with whom we share a relationship exactly where they stand with us: what they are doing well and where we believe they are falling short in order for them to increase their playing time or bring home a larger Christmas bonus? Thankfully, we can and should be both. It isn't nice *or* kind. Commit to being nice *and* kind.

21

How to Be Kind

FRIENDS ARE NICE. Great teammates are kind. Don't confuse nice with kind. Nice is saying "great job." Kind is demanding the highest standard out of our ourselves first and then our teammates. The following is how we do so.

An Inverse Relation Between Timing and Tone and Volume

When holding teammates accountable, there should be an inverse ratio between level of adversity and our tone and volume. The greater the adversity, the softer the tone and lower the volume.

When providing accountability during a battle, or any emotionally charged event, speak in a softer tone and lower volume. Yelling or screaming at a teammate during an already emotionally charged event will rarely be well received or acted upon. As discussed, no one likes being told they are falling short at any time and especially so when it is being screamed at them. Further, if we find ourselves yelling or screaming at a teammate who is not meeting the organization's standards, it is probably our own fault, in that we have let it continue to this point of frustration. We have seen them falling short for weeks, perhaps months, yet we said nothing. If we had addressed it immediately, we would not be having these same levels of anger and frustration about teammates not meeting the standard.

When being held accountable, take a few deep breaths to control your heart rate. The time this takes should afford you the opportunity to think about how you would like to respond in order for the team to best accomplish the mission. We suggest making it a habit to simply respond with "yes." After the battle is over, if your feelings were hurt enough that it would lead to a deterioration in the relationship with your teammate, go and speak to them at that time.

Screaming at a teammate is not "holding them accountable." Doing so in a location, tone, and volume that allows teammates an opportunity to reflect on that feedback and make a positive change for the better is. Accountability is not simply about telling our teammates what to do better; it is ensuring that we are doing so in a manner that allows them to do so.

Be Positive and Be Specific!

We must hold teammates accountable when they are not meeting our organization's standards, but we must remember to take every opportunity to also do so when teammates meet the standards. It happens much more frequently than not, and our recognition of it is vitally important to mission success. Telling a teammate that we appreciate their attention to detail, hard work, punctuality, or great hustle, is more likely to reinforce the behaviors that we want than will highlighting the behaviors that we don't want. Furthermore, that teammate will be more likely to take our "negative" accountability more constructively when we correct them for a poor choice later. Also, be specific with both praise and constructive feedback. "Good job" is no more helpful than "do better." Delete "good job" from your vernacular. Instead, recognize the specific behaviors that teammates are exhibiting that are helping the team accomplish its mission.

When we are being praised by a coach or fellow teammate for behavior that is helping the team accomplish its mission, we should thank them. We must especially remember to do so when they are giving us feedback on how to better meet standards, which is much more difficult for a teammate to provide. If they do so, they are giving a clear message that they care more about us (and the team) than they care about their own discomfort in providing that feedback.

Kind teammates hold teammates accountable when they are not meeting the standard. When doing so, provide specific feedback on what they are doing that is hurting the team and what they can do to improve it. Never miss an opportunity, though, to hold teammates accountable when they are meeting the standard. Provide specific feedback on what they are doing well and how it is helping the team accomplish its mission.

22

Wash Your Hands! Developing a Culture of Accountability

"WASH YOUR HANDS!" Most of us have heard this refrain thousands of times throughout our childhoods. We were made to do so by parents who simply could not imagine our sitting down to eat after we had played outside all day long without first doing so. Our hands were dirty; they were covered in sweat and grime. Knuckles were scraped and bleeding after falls from our bikes. We had sand and mud stuck deep under our fingernails. Washing hands is one of the most important and effective ways to avoid getting sick or spreading germs.[1]

For Eric Kapitulik, the message remains the same, but the deliverer has changed. Eric's wife now tells him to do so every time after feeding their chickens. Washing our hands takes some effort and time. It would be easier and quicker if we didn't do it, but doing so makes us, and the team, healthier. As any parent knows, when one child gets sick, the whole family gets sick.

Many individuals will not willingly hold a teammate accountable. For most of us, it is easier to say nothing, to just sit down at the table and start eating despite the dirt and grime. Parents must at times force hands to be washed, but they make it easy to do so. As children, we

---

[1] https://www.cdc.gov/handwashing/why-handwashing.html.

may not enjoy doing it, but at the very least, we accept it. Eventually, we even come to realize that the person demanding it has both our and the family's best interest at heart; they are ensuring that all family members are as healthy as possible.

Accountability, like washing our hands, ensures the same. As with hand washing, creating a *culture of accountability* takes effort, but without it, sickness or disease will spread through our team. Many leaders complain that their people don't hold one another accountable. To establish and sustain a culture of accountability, instead of complaining about it, be like the parent who makes us wash our hands. Make us do so, but make it easy.

Conduct regularly scheduled debriefs upon completion (or sooner, if the team or mission requires it) of any project or event, whether it's an athletic contest, school play, or business quarter. Leaders must make it a habit to conduct a regularly scheduled washing-of-the-hands. All aspects of the event are discussed. *What* went well? What didn't? More specifically, what helped or didn't help our team accomplish the mission? What do we need to continue to do and what do we need to change in order to accomplish our mission more quickly, more efficiently, and more profitably in the future? We then discuss *who* did well, who didn't, and what we/they need to continue or need to change. These regularly scheduled debriefs, or washing-of-the-hands, are not about finding fault or assigning blame. They are about getting better.

If possible, all teammates should take notes throughout the evaluation period to ensure that opportunities for both continuation and improvement are not forgotten prior to the washing. If unable (i.e., an athlete can't take notes during practice or a game), they are at least aware to take mental notes.

A few guidelines for conducting a "washing of the hands":

1. Communicate to every member of your team that upon completion of a given event or period of time a "washing" (debriefing) will occur and to come prepared for it. This should happen as soon as possible after the event, but allow team members to emotionally "cool off."

2. All teammates show up on time, preferably with a pen and notebook.

3. The leader facilitates the "washing" to ensure areas of discussion are not missed. However, a general rule is that a leader who is speaking more than everyone else in the room should stop. The leader should ask questions, but the team should be discussing the event. Other than making sure areas of evaluation aren't missed and asking questions to get at the root of issues, the leader should ensure that the tone of feedback remains focused on *getting better*, rather than on *finding blame*.

4. Teammates provide feedback on every section of the project and on every teammate involved, including the leader.

5. Team leaders are evaluated just as any other member of their team is evaluated. While doing so, team leaders have a great opportunity to show the rest of the team how to receive feedback, which is just as important as how to provide it. Be positive and not argumentative. Thank them for providing it because it makes you and the whole team better.

6. At the end of every "washing", every member of the team is asked to review with the team what went well, what didn't, what they did well, and what and how they will improve. This ensures that all team members understand what they and the team need to continue to do, and areas requiring improvement.

Many readers might think that this takes a lot of time. It does in the short term. In the long run, it saves even more. Superior performances and behaviors are recognized and celebrated, ensuring a continuance of it. Destructive performances and behaviors are also addressed and corrected, helping to ensure that the same time-consuming mistakes aren't allowed to continue.

Very few people voluntarily seek out personal confrontation. It makes us extremely uncomfortable. It is difficult to hold anyone accountable, let alone a teammate who might be older or a higher performer than us. A parent makes us wash our hands *for* our and the family's benefit. A mandatory and very thorough debrief after every project or event helps our team become more comfortable with providing feedback *to* one another because they will come to understand that they are providing feedback *for* one another. Eventually, this will also make them more comfortable providing and receiving feedback *for* their teammates on a more regular basis, creating a culture of accountability.

23

Do Not "Lead by Example"

ACROSS NORTH AMERICA, parents, teachers, coaches, business leaders, and everyone else wants to tell us about a teammate who "leads by example." We are told, "They prepare as best as they can. They show up every day on time and they stay late. They give 100% and they *perform* when it's their time to perform. But they don't say much. They are quiet. They lead by example."

Often, after working with these individuals, we were not overly impressed with their leadership abilities. What we typically saw were teammates who met or exceeded the standards at near-superhuman levels. They held themselves to incredibly high standards and then were told that they were thus "leading by example."

Meanwhile, a teammate right next to them was cutting corners, not working hard, displaying a poor attitude, not meeting any standards of the organization—and they said nothing! Silence is consent. If we say nothing, we are implicitly agreeing with those behaviors.

Wind technicians repair wind turbines that run huge wind farms for renewable energy. These turbines are incredibly powerful and dangerous, so technicians have a checklist to follow to ensure safety. Turbines are repaired in burning heat and frigid cold, in the rain and the mud. Technicians get tired, frustrated, and stressed. They start to rush and don't follow their safety checklists (a standard).

Turbines are also typically located in remote locations far from site managers. Two technicians always work together. If one sees the safety standard not being met and says nothing, that person is silently consenting.

If "leading by example" merely means that we prepare as best as we can, give 100% every day, and perform when it is our time to perform, then there is no true thing as leading by example. When we question clients if they think anyone deserves "special credit" for doing these things, they respond, "No, they are *doing their job.*" In our vernacular, we call it meeting the standard (if those are standards for your team). Great teammates do it first and we want to recognize them for doing so—just not by telling them that they are "leading by example." Admittedly, if we can't meet the standard, we will never be a leader, but we aren't *leading* just because we meet or exceed the standards. As leaders and teammates of those individuals, we must recognize them. A team of them would take over the world!

However, the way most parents, teachers, coaches, and business leaders talk about "leading by example," they are discussing someone who meets the standard and is desperately hoping that their teammates will do so too. Unfortunately, hope is not a strategy. Very few teams, if any, are comprised of individuals who all meet the standards, every day, and in everything they do. Mistakes happen. Det 1 was arguably one of the finest Marine Corps units ever assembled. It was a team of incredibly talented, tough, professional, and dedicated officers and enlisted Marines. There were still instances of standards not being met. A failure to do so, combined with a failure to hold teammates accountable during Det 1's preparation for Operation Ricochet, had deadly consequences during their execution phase.

The same occurs to our own teams, although thankfully not with such horrifying consequences. The Program is incredibly fortunate and privileged to work with some of the greatest collegiate and professional athletic teams and corporations throughout North America. These teams are filled with exceptionally hard-working, smart, and talented individuals who consistently meet the standards. On those same teams are individuals who do not, and even those who do, get complacent.

A preparation phase rarely has deadly consequences. Prior to the fixing of a turbine or conducting Operation Ricochet, no one dies. The same is true in a figurative sense for athletic teams during practice and pharmaceutical companies prior to launching a new drug. No one suffers life-threatening consequences then. We must never forget, however, that there is always an execution phase, during which Det 1 Marines and wind technicians are horribly injured or worse. Athletes and coaches suffer the pain of losing the game or a disappointing season. Business leaders fall short of their budgetary requirements, people lose their jobs, and companies go out of business. Thankfully, the opposite is true when teammates understand the fallacy of "leading by example." Instead, by meeting the standards and then holding their teammates accountable to doing so, great teammates ensure those "deadly" consequences never occur and teams accomplish their mission.

Det 1 Assault Team Corpsman Tim Bryan was standing with Jamey in the stack waiting to enter the crisis site. When both the breacher and their other Det 1 teammate were wounded, Doc Bryan immediately told two other Marines to "get out of the stack" in order to help evacuate their wounded comrades. Doc Bryan didn't just pick up his wounded teammates and *hope* that other Marines would help as well. He selected two and *told* them to do so. They did so without hesitation, but they still needed to be told first.

During training, Jamey and his teammates didn't work hard and then *hope* that their teammates did as well. They held one another accountable, forced one another out of their comfort zones, and made one another better every single day. Every workout, every high-altitude jump, and every training scenario was debriefed in some form. Individuals took pride in their own performance and even more so in that of their fellow teammates. They made it a habit to tell teammates what they did well, but also what they could do to improve. Because of this, after their initial setback with the failed breach, Det 1 was able to quickly recover their momentum and attack with precision and overwhelming fire superiority, ending in the successful capture of the IED maker.

A world-class soldier, sailor, marine, or airman is one who holds himself or herself to the highest possible standards. The same is true for an athlete, student, or corporate employee. A world-class military, athletic, or corporate *team* has men and women who do that too, but they also demand and help their teammates to do so, as well.

Stop "leading by example." Instead, be a great teammate: meet the standards and then demand and help your teammates to do the same.

Stop "leading by example." Instead, be a great teammate: meet the standards and then demand and help your teammates to do the same.

24

Consistency Builds Trust

TRUST IS THE foundation of every relationship. Our teammates deserve to know how we will behave not just when things are going well, but, most importantly, when they are not. They need to trust us, and vice versa. If not, our relationship will have a poor foundation. Unfortunately, teammates, and team leaders alike, destroy that trust constantly in ways that can be avoided.

A corporate teammate who produces an excellent product on Monday but then turns in substandard work on Wednesday destroys trust. A business partner or teammate who does their assigned tasks only some of the time destroys trust. A football player who goes hard on first down, but then takes second down off, or a softball player focused during one at-bat, but not the next, destroys trust. Teammates, and team leaders, have no idea who they are going to get, and hence, what they are going to get. Consistent behavior is predictive of consistent performance. Consistency is key.

By the middle of their deployment, Det 1 had experienced much success. They had conducted several successful direct-action raids. They had become very proficient with the method in which they breached and attacked through the crisis site. Prior to deployment, Det 1 had practiced the same mission hundreds of times over thousands of hours of training. Each Marine had a job to do and standards to meet every single time. Throughout their training and during earlier successful operations in Iraq, the breacher had blown the door in and

Marines immediately "rode" that chaos and confusion into the crisis site with a violence of action, never allowing any return enemy fire.

Operation Ricochet was very different. Most of Det 1's assaulting force had been thrown to the ground from the blast. They immediately started receiving intense enemy fire. Teammates had been shot and were bleeding profusely everywhere. The "bad guys" on the other side of the door knew the Marines had landed and were going to be entering the front door. Their fire concentrated on that area. The lead two Marines in the stack stepped into that area and through it, trusting implicitly that their teammates would follow them as they had hundreds of times prior.

Trust allowed them to do so. It allows the Det 1 Marines and us to stay focused on the mission and our competition, rather than worry about our own teammates following us through the door—or not. If a teammate always hands work in on time and without error and has done so throughout our relationship, we trust that that teammate will do so again. We trust that those who have behaved in a "cool, calm, and collected" manner during times of adversity will do so again. If a member of a hockey team's penalty-killing unit consistently "sells out" and gives up their body to stop a shot, we know that the next time we're on the ice together, that teammate will do so again. We can all stay focused on accomplishing the mission rather than an inconsistent teammate.

The opposite occurs on bad teams. A shooting guard sometimes works hard on defense and then other times does not. This forces teammates to "cheat over" to help with the guard's missed assignments on every possession. The defense breaks down and the other team scores easily. Every corporation in America has countless examples of leaders giving more work as well as the "really important" work to a small group of individuals on the team whom they trust implicitly. Those trusted individuals ultimately leave the team because of the unreasonable and unnecessary workload, and the organization suffers.

As discussed, consistency is key, for both the teammates meeting the standard and for those holding them accountable to it. We lose trust if we hold different teammates accountable to different standards or if we enforce standards inconsistently. Sometimes it is tempting to be inconsistent and let our standards slip. It is indeed more challenging to hold the best player on an athletic team, or the best salesperson on a corporate team, accountable. Performance matters, and losing that production even for a short time can cause us to lose games or not make budget.

Admittedly, when The Program works with teams and organizations there are times when our leadership instructors want to let "little things" go. We like the team with whom we are working. They make a mental mistake, they fail to touch the line on a sprint, or use the wrong commands during an exercise. They are working so hard and displaying such a great attitude. Our instructors, like all teammates and team leaders, want to pretend that they didn't notice the mistake or talk themselves into believing that maybe they didn't see the mistake occur. However, we know that if we don't hold the individual and team accountable, even though they may indeed "like" us more in that moment, they will lose trust in us. We remind parents about this constantly. All teammates would do well to remember it as well.

We must have one team and one set of standards, all the time for everyone. This is not to say that consequences are not different for different team members, based on a host of factors, but there is one set of standards for everyone all the time and a consequence for not meeting them. Most importantly, there is not one standard for some and another for others. Holding different teammates to different standards based on an individual's talent level is the surest way to decrease the team's performance. Maybe it won't suffer in the next game or the next month, but eventually it will, typically when the lights are brightest.

Having inconsistent standards, inconsistently meeting them, and inconsistently holding our teammates accountable to them undermines trust in teammates, team leaders, and the organization. It guarantees cracks in its foundation, destroys relationships, and ensures a deterioration in our culture and performance. Thankfully, the opposite is true as well. Having consistent standards, consistently meeting them, consistently holding teammates accountable when they meet them and when they do not, and consistently enforcing a consequence for the latter and a benefit for the former, all assure a strong foundation, deeper relationships, a strengthening of an organization's culture, and an increase in consistent performance.

Individuals can win games, but great teams compete for championships. Great teams are composed of great teammates and great team leaders. Great teammates meet the standards first. Consistently. Then they hold their teammates accountable to doing the same. Consistently.

25

Friend or Teammate?

WE GO TO the movies with good friends. We go to battle with great teammates. The Program considers a friend anyone who is a good person with whom we enjoy spending our time (a "good" person doesn't lie, cheat, or steal). A teammate is a member of our organization with whom we accomplish a mission. Friends are held to two standards: be a good person and be enjoyable to spend time with. Teammates are held to two standards as well: meet our organization's standards and then hold our teammates accountable to achieving them.

We go to the movies with good friends. We go to battle with great teammates.

There are very few people who don't desire to be well liked—some more than others, but we all have an ego. If you don't think you do, right now, go and find a group photo that you are in. Look at it. Answer the following question truthfully: Who did you look for first?

Not only do we want to be well *liked*, we want to be loved! For many individuals on a team, some of whom are even high performers, this desire to be popular, to be a good friend to everyone, is more important than being a great teammate who meets the standard and then holds their teammates accountable to doing so. Holding a teammate accountable is uncomfortable. When we hold some teammates accountable, it can upset them, make them angry at us, or even cause them not to like us or want to be friends with us.

Almost every organization has people who are very popular, whom everyone likes a lot. They get along great with everyone. The Program works with numerous teams whose members are all great friends. Team cohesion is their greatest strength. It is also their greatest weakness. Great team cohesion is a team's greatest weakness when the value of being great friends, of "getting along," supersedes the value of being great teammates, of "getting better."

We only grow as individuals, and as a team, when we are outside of our *comfort zone*. Great teammates meet their organization's standards and then hold their teammates accountable to doing the same. That is challenging to do. It's outside almost all our comfort zones. At times, it might make for an uncomfortable workplace environment. Being uncomfortable is where we grow as individuals and as a team though. It is where and when we "get better."

Team cohesion is important, but not more than helping to make each other better. We need to be great teammates on every team we are fortunate to be a part of. We may never face explosive charges blowing us up or actual bullets being shot at us, but every team will face adversity; we will all have to go to battle in some form. Great teammates ensure that we not only survive it, but are better for the experience, first by meeting the standards and then by holding all teammates accountable to meeting them, as well. It is how we make each other the best versions of ourselves for the battlefields on which we fight.

Thankfully, we can and should be both good friends and great teammates. Holding teammates accountable doesn't have to be incendiary. It shouldn't fracture a relationship. It may very well upset one or both individuals in the relationship, but not fracture it. As discussed earlier, trust that our teammates are holding us accountable because our (and the team's) improvement is of the utmost importance to them. Hold teammates accountable because their (and our) team becoming the best version of themselves is more important than our discomfort while doing so.

It is easy to be a friend, to be a good person, and for people to enjoy spending time with us. It is incredibly challenging to be a great teammate, to meet the standards and then hold our teammates accountable to achieving them as well. We can be both, but which is more important to us?

Everyone is a hero when it is seventy degrees and sunny. We are all good friends when things are going well, but we need great teammates (and great team leaders) when it's not! We *hope* for seventy degrees and sunny, but hope is not a strategy. We must plan and prepare, knowing that it will not be. We do so by making a commitment to be a great teammate above all else.

We go to the movies with good friends. We go to battle with great teammates.

Action Items on Holding Teammates Accountable

1. Nice is saying hello, please, and thank you. Nice is sitting down with a lonely classmate or co-worker. Be nice!
2. Kind is holding a teammate accountable. We understand that it may hurt their feelings or make them upset at us, but because it will make them (and our team) better, kind people hold teammates accountable. Be nice *and* kind!
3. Silence is neither being nice nor kind. Silence is consent. We stay silent because we lack moral courage. Don't! If our teammates (in our school, on the athletic field, in our business, or in our American society) are doing something wrong or falling short of that team's standards, say something! Have moral courage.
4. When holding a teammate accountable, there is an inverse relationship between level of adversity and tone/volume. Typically, the greater the adversity or stress, the softer the tone and the lower the volume should be to be more effective in ensuring our teammate's improvement.
5. Be positive and be specific. Telling our teammates specifically what behaviors are helping our team succeed and when they are exhibiting them are as impactful, if not more so, as highlighting what and when they are not.
6. Standardize accountability. Most individuals will not take it upon themselves to hold a teammate accountable. Instead, make it systemic to the organization. Set up a regularly

scheduled "washing of the hands" when every member of the team comes prepared with feedback for all other team members and the organization.

7. Do *not* "lead by example." Typically, someone who does this is meeting (or exceeding) that organization's standards. That's the first standard of being a great teammate. Now, accomplish the second: hold your teammates accountable to doing the same.

8. Be consistent! Hold all teammates—including our best players and highest-grossing salespeople—accountable to meeting the standards. Enforce a consequence. Picking and choosing what standards, when, and with whom to hold accountable will undermine trust among teammates, with team leaders, and throughout the organization. A decrease in performance follows soon after.

9. Friend or teammate? A friend is a good person with whom we enjoy spending our time. It is easy to be a good friend. A teammate meets our organization's standards and then demands and helps their teammates to do the same. It is challenging to be a great teammate. Accept the challenge and be both!

10. Regardless of how often we may have held a teammate accountable in the past for failing to meet a standard, if it is still not being met, we must do so again and again. And again. Our standards are worn down an inch at a time. The moment we allow someone on our team not to meet the standards, that becomes the new standard. **The standard we walk past is the new standard we set.**

Saved Rounds on Holding Teammates Accountable

Organizations always *talk* about what is important. What teams *recognize* is what actually *is* important.

Every Sunday morning, in winter, at 7:45 a.m., Eric, his wife Melissa, and their son Axel stop at the Dunkin' Donuts in their hometown on their way to Axel's hockey practice. They purchase five chocolate glazed Munchkins. Prior to the start of practice, they review with him how he can "earn" each Munchkin: the first is for continuing to go hard once he becomes tired, the second is for giving his 100% in everything that he does (i.e., sprinting to and from a sip of water during a water break is as important as giving 100% during a drill), the third is for making it fun (not for *having* fun, but rather for *making* it fun: it is his job to make it fun, not the coaches' job for him to have it), and the fourth for saying "please" and "thank you" (for being a gentleman). Right now, they believe these standards reinforce their Core Values of Selflessness, Toughness, and Discipline.

These are also the standards for Axel at football, wrestling, lacrosse, and Ultimate Obstacles, the indoor obstacle course Axel attends while becoming a "ninja." These are also his standards at guitar practice. Most importantly, they are Team Kapitulik's standards in school and in life. These need not be the standards for your children, athletes, or corporate teammates. Every leader, every team, and every battlefield is different. What each leader finds important and critical for their team's ability to consistently accomplish its mission will also be different. Selflessness, Toughness, and Discipline matter for Team Kapitulik. Axel's willingness to meet those standards that reinforce these Core Values will ensure his and the team's opportunity to compete for championships and accomplish their own missions on whatever battlefields they choose to compete. Team Kapitulik's standards may not be right for your team, but something must be. Whatever those things are for your team, clearly define and then recognize them!

On the drive home after practice, Axel will immediately ask if they can "do the donuts."

Eric pulls the first Munchkin out of the bag and asks Axel what it is for; he responds, "For being tough." Eric asks him what it means to be tough; he responds, "When you are tired, you keep going . . . and you do it with a good attitude." Eric then asks Melissa if Axel was tough. She provides feedback to Axel. Eric then asks Axel the same question and gives him an opportunity to tell Eric and his wife if he thought he was tough. Finally, Eric provides a few examples of how he was (or wasn't) tough. If he was tough, Eric hands him the Munchkin, which Axel promptly eats in one bite. If not tough, Axel doesn't get the Munchkin. If we "give the Munchkin" every time regardless of whether Axel (or your own teammate) is or isn't tough, we as the leaders render the reward meaningless. Our children know this. Why do so few parents?[1]

Eric and his wife repeat this process for the next three Munchkins. When they get to the fifth Munchkin, Eric asks Axel what the fifth one is for. He responds without hesitation, "Because my mom and dad love me so much." Eric explains to Axel that the first four Munchkins make them proud and he must earn that, but the fifth one he will always get, because regardless of who he is or isn't, regardless of what he does or doesn't do, his mom and dad will *always* love him with their whole body and soul.

Next, if Axel wants to talk about his performance, they will talk about how he played, but only if he brings it up. They don't

---

[1] We are often asked about our thoughts on "participation trophies." Our response usually surprises most people. A "participation" trophy is not meaningless. As its name would imply, a participation trophy recognizes a child who *participated* on the team. Warriors and MVPs don't want participation trophies. It is insulting to them, but not everybody is a warrior or an MVP. What level of participation is required to receive a participation trophy renders it more or less meaningful, not the act of giving or receiving it. A much greater issue is when a team doesn't recognize their MVP because it *might* hurt the feelings of everyone else who is only being recognized for their participation. Finally, The Program believes that the apocalypse is upon us when parents and coaches start to give "MVP trophies" to everyone on the team. In the interim, go ahead and recognize everyone for their participation.

really care how he *plays*. They care about how he *behaves*. Teachers, coaches, and business leaders should care about both. Many do, but unfortunately, many do not. Some care much more about performance than behavior. Even more unfortunate is that in the short term, it can work; we can win a lot of games and even a championship on talent or performance alone. However, to do so on a consistent basis, both must be a priority.

The chance that Axel earns a scholarship to play at the collegiate level is incredibly small. The chance that he earns a living playing a sport that he loves is even smaller. However, he *can* earn the first four Munchkins every day of his life by just choosing to do so. Talk about what is important to us and therefore important for our organization's ability to accomplish its mission. However, the team will know that what we recognize is what *is* important. We must do so as leaders of our teams, but it is even more impactful when our teammates recognize us. In any event, Axel will always get the fifth donut from his parents.

Organizations always *talk* about what is important. What teams *recognize* is what *is* important. Recognize and reward good performance. Recognize and reward good behavior more. And always remember to give a fifth donut. . . .

SECTION

III

Team Leaders

A HIGH-PITCHED WHINING SOUND followed by a bang a few seconds later means a bullet is traveling in your general direction. In a firefight, due to the intensity and volume of bullets flying back and forth, these sounds become like white noise, swallowed by all the other sounds of battle. But a *crack* gets your attention—it means that a bullet just missed your head.

As they drew closer to the Iraqi Police station, the *cracks* increased in such frequency and volume that it sounded like popcorn popping. And Mac and his Marines knew that it was no longer a wild goose chase....

U.S. Marines during the Battle of Najaf.

Note: Photo courtesy of Lucian Read.

87

26

Wild-Goose Chase

IN THE SUMMER of 2004, Jake "Mac" MacDonald returned to Iraq for his second deployment. His unit was tasked with restoring peace to the city of An Najaf. A cleric named Muqtada al-Sadr had taken control of the famed city. Using his death squads and fighters from the Mahdi militia, al-Sadr imposed draconian laws on the populace, intimidated local business owners, and tortured and murdered Iraqi policemen and anybody else who supported the Iraqi or US governments.

Najaf is home to the Imam Ali Mosque and is considered by Muslim Shias to be the third holiest city, ranking behind only Mecca and Medina. In order to restore peace to Najaf, it would be necessary to remove al-Sadr from power and return the mosque to the people. Knowing this, Muqtada marshalled his sizable forces inside and directly around the mosque, using one of their holiest sites to stage their attacks.

Mac's leaders decided that it would not be good for public perception to have American forces kicking down the door of the Imam Ali Mosque. Instead, their original plan was to train the local Iraqi police and army until they were competent enough to take back their own city. For the first few weeks of their deployment, the Marines formed an uneasy truce with al-Sadr forces. Al-Sadr's militia was concentrated in an area called the Old City around the Imam Ali Mosque. The truce was fairly straightforward: the American forces wouldn't go into al-Sadr's forces' area and they wouldn't come out of it. This truce lasted for a few brief weeks before one of the bloodiest and most violent battles of the Iraq War broke out.

Mac was the commander for the 11th Marine Expeditionary Unit's Light Armored Reconnaissance platoon. Essentially, he was in charge of five light armored vehicles (imagine tanks with wheels) and 31 Marines. The night before the Battle of Najaf officially started, Mac's unit was tasked with executing a reconnaissance and surveillance mission into the Old City and the Najaf cemetery, the Wadi-us-Salaam. This is the largest cemetery in the world, covering nearly 1500 acres. To the Western eye, the cemetery bears almost no resemblance to one we would be accustomed. The layout appears haphazard, filled with meandering paths between ancient tombstones, and massive underground crypts often linked by underground tunnels. Mac's platoon inserted into the cemetery under the cover of darkness. With their thermal optics, they could see deep into both the cemetery and the Old City. It was their mission to observe and report on any enemy activity in either area.

In the early morning hours of August 4, 2004, Mac and his Marines saw tracer fire arc across the sky on the other side of the cemetery, followed shortly thereafter by the distinctive *rat-ta-tat* sound of machine-gun fire. Mac and his Marines knew that there was an Iraqi police station in the area where the fire was concentrated. The intensity and volume of the machine-gun fire increased. Knowing that they were only minutes away and in a position to support the Iraqi police station, Mac called it in on the radio and offered to assist. They were told to hold their positions and continue to observe. The fighting eventually died down, only to resume an hour later with renewed ferocity. This time, in addition to the machine-gun fire, they could also see rocket-propelled grenades streaking toward the police station. Again, they called it in and offered to assist. Again, they were told to hold their position. By this time, the sun was beginning to crest the horizon. Knowing that they would no longer be able to remain unseen during daylight hours, Mac's unit returned to their base.

The end of a mission does not signify the end of a workday, though. Before Marines even think about taking care of their personal needs (shower, food, rest), they must make sure their gear is taken care of. This means both refueling their vehicles and rearming them. They must also clean their personal weapons and make sure that the rest of their gear and equipment is ready to be used at a moment's notice. In addition, Mac also had to debrief the Intelligence section on everything that they had seen or done during their earlier mission. At this point, Mac and his Marines had been awake for 24 hours. Mac was finally able to return to his tent to try to get some sleep. Sitting on his cot, Mac had barely begun to unlace his boots when he received a message from his radio operator.

"Pale Rider 6 wants to talk to you," the Marine told him.

Pale Rider was the callsign for Mac's parent unit and the designator of 6 signified that it was his boss, the battalion commander. He informed them that the Iraqi police station was being attacked again and that they would be one of the units tasked with helping the police. Mac yelled, "Mount up!" and called for his vehicle commanders. Even though some of Mac's Marines, after being awake for more than 24 hours, had only been asleep for 30 minutes, they didn't need any extra motivation to get going. The promise of a firefight sharpened their focus and filled them with nervous energy. Approximately half of Mac's Marines were with him during the initial invasion of Iraq less than a year earlier. They had already seen combat and knew firsthand the chaos that it wrought. However, most of the younger Marines had only joined the Marine Corps after the invasion. This was to be their first time in combat and would be a chance to test their mettle.

A few minutes later, they rolled out of base, weapons loaded and adrenaline coursing through their veins. They reached the Iraqi police station ready to fight. The Marines looked around and saw … nothing. No machine-gun fire. No RPGs. No bad guys. They circled the area, making sure no enemy fighters were present, and then received the order to return to base. They again serviced their vehicles and cleaned their personal weapons. Again, Mac debriefed the intelligence section on what little he saw. By this point, they had been awake for nearly 30 hours. Mac returned to his tent and laid down on his cot without even bothering to take his boots off. Just as he pulled his sleeping bag over himself, Mac's radio operator again entered the tent.

"We are going out again, Sir. The police station is being attacked."

Mac called for his Marines to get up and get on the vehicles, but now the atmosphere was much different. Whereas the first time his Marines were primed and ready to fight, they now felt that they were being called out on a wild-goose chase that would only delay their sleep even longer. Fortunately, Mac had some great subordinate leaders and teammates who, through their words, actions, and body language, forced the Marines to take it seriously, even if they didn't feel it themselves.

It was still quiet on the drive down to the police station. Mac then heard a single popping noise through his hearing protection. Few people may know this, but gunfire sounds different depending on which way it is going. When you pull the trigger, gun powder is ignited, there is a mini explosion, and the resulting gasses push the bullet out of the barrel. This creates a bang. A high-pitched whine followed by a bang a few seconds later means a bullet is traveling in your general direction. Due to the speed it is traveling, a bullet creates a sonic boom as it moves through the air, producing a loud cracking or snapping noise. Hearing the crack means that you are within the sonic boom. The *bangs* and *whines* blend into the other frenzied sounds of war, but the *crack* gets your attention—it means a bullet just missed your head.

As they drew closer to the Iraqi police station, the *crack* sounds increased in frequency until it sounded like popcorn popping. When Mac heard the bullets striking the side of his vehicle, he knew that it was no longer a wild-goose chase.

Very few professions require their people to be on call 24 hours a day. However, we need leaders who are prepared for anything, at any time. Mac's Marines were some of the most honorable, courageous, and committed with whom he had ever served. However, even they needed great leadership to reach their potential and accomplish their mission, and he needed them. The Battle of Najaf was one of the most violent, hard-fought battles of the Iraq War. That the Marines were able to come away from it victorious was a reflection on their incredible talent and embodiment of the Marine Corps Core Values (Honor, Courage, and Commitment), their unit's extremely high goals and standards, and their commitment to them. Mac and his Marines were part of a world-class culture.

They fought for 36 hours straight, having already been awake for over 30 hours, and having dealt with multiple setbacks and false alarms. They were able to do this because of that world-class culture and because they were both great teammates and great team leaders.

As previously highlighted, everyone is a hero when it is seventy degrees and sunny with a slight breeze blowing in off the coast. Unfortunately, that is not when you need them. We need great teammates and great leaders when it's not!

Some military units are very good. And some are not. The difference is their unit's culture and the great teammates and great team leaders that fill its ranks. We have already discussed culture and teammates and how we define and develop each. Now, we turn to defining and developing great team leaders.

27

What Is and Isn't Leadership, and Who Are and Aren't Leaders?

TEAM LEADERS ARE held to two standards: *Accomplish the mission, and take care of your teammates.* Great team leaders are those who consistently do so.

We will discuss these standards in much greater detail in the following chapters. They are incredibly powerful and their achievement is critical to any organization's long-term success, but before discussing them, we must first define what is and what isn't leadership and who are and who aren't leaders. Most of us can't do so, which unfortunately ensures that individuals who should not be in vitally important leadership roles are nevertheless placed there. More egregious, our inability to effectively define true leadership, and to determine what individuals should be developed and selected for even greater responsibility, leads to mission failure, and ultimately to the collapse of entire organizations.

Best-selling author and leadership expert John Maxwell famously wrote, "Leadership can be defined by one word—influence." Influence is leadership, but it does not necessarily make you a leader. A leader has the desire and ability to use that *influence* on those around them.

Very few people, of any age, understand this. During any televised sporting event, announcers will inevitably praise the highest-scoring athlete, as they score more and more points, for "the great leadership they are showing." The same is true in our schools: teachers and principals consistently praise their smartest students for their *leadership*. In corporate America, CEOs and presidents highlight the *leadership* of their top-grossing salespeople.

Furthermore, the most prolific scorer, the smartest student, and the highest-grossing salesperson are all anointed as the *leader* because of their performance. This is a mistake. Although they *are* exceptional athletes, students, and salespeople, and have influence because of it, they often lack a desire or an ability to be a leader—both of which are required to be one.

Many coaches and corporate bosses fail to remember this. We all *want* our best performers to be our best leaders, but unless those highest performers have the desire and ability, they will never be leaders. As leaders, we compound this mistake when we *force* them into a leadership role. This inevitably leads to frustration in both parties, and often to a decrease in the individual's performance.

Unfortunately, we have seen this occur countless times. Coaches make their highest scorer a captain and then demand the person act like a leader. Instead they not only don't do so, they also stop scoring as much. Parents and school administrators force young people into leadership roles in their school and their grades suffer.[1] Corporate presidents tend to promote their best salespeople to regional sales director, and their individual sales—as well as the entire region's sales—drop immediately.

Furthermore, we gain influence (leadership) in one of two ways: through our title and through who we are (our Core Values, our personality, our work ethic, our talent, our intelligence, etc.). All things being equal (which they rarely are), a captain in the Marine Corps has more influence than a private, a head coach has more influence

---

[1] The Program is unaware of when parents began reinforcing with their children that being a great teammate was somehow less impressive and less desirable than being a great leader. If The Program staff's children grow up to be the best teammates in the world, every member of the staff would be incredibly proud of it. We are not sure why it seems that so many parents wouldn't be.

than an assistant coach, and a CEO has more influence than a regional director. Even though *who we are* gives us far more influence, titles do matter. Giving someone a title will give them more influence. That can be a great thing if they use that additional influence positively. It can also be very bad if they use it negatively. We must always remember to ask ourselves: if we promote, do we truly want that individual to have the greater influence that comes with the title?

You may have someone in your organization who does not meet any of the standards of a leader discussed later in this section, but they are influential and they have a desire and ability to use that influence. Typically, their influence stems from their talent and their ability is based on their charismatic personality. Maybe they know where the best party is on Saturday night. A parent, head coach, principal, or CEO may not consider them a leader, but their peers follow them. As leaders of our organizations, we must recognize that such people are leaders, despite our desire that they not be. They may be leading our team in the wrong direction, but they are still leaders. If you don't want them to be leaders on your team, either you change them drastically, or you get rid of them. Coaches and corporate presidents can choose individuals on their team to fill certain leadership roles and provide the corresponding titles (Team Captain, Regional Director, etc.). The team decides who the leaders are, though. Individuals who don't embody our team's culture are *dangerous* to mission accomplishment. If they also have a desire and ability to negatively influence other members of the team, they are *deadly*.

In the Marine Corps, our superiors provide us with fitness reports throughout our careers that serve as performance reviews. One of the blocks in the fitness report is the "Billet Description," a basic description of the current job you are performing. The first line of any leader's billet description is always "responsible for everything that happens or fails to happen in their unit."

Now that we have described what is and isn't leadership and who is and isn't a leader, we must highlight the two standards to which team leaders are held: (1) accomplish the mission, and (2) take care of your teammates. Both will be discussed in great depth after an explanation of what exactly a "mission" is.

28

The Mission

THE FIRST STANDARD to which a leader is held is mission accomplishment. It is an expectation that this is accomplished legally and with high personal and team standards of behavior. As discussed previously, consistently meeting (and exceeding) our organization's standards that reinforce our Core Values should ensure long-term consistent performance. The opposite is also true. A disregard for our Core Values and the standards and consequences that reinforce them ensures a decrease in our organization's ability to accomplish its mission.

Furthermore, if behaviors are immoral or illegal, they will eventually result in any leader's eventual downfall, and typically also that of the team they lead. There are numerous high-profile examples of exactly this occurring in collegiate and professional sports as well as in corporate America.

We must stay focused on our behaviors, but as leaders (and teammates) we must also always be aware of our performance, of what we are here to do, of our mission. Leaders who are unable to lead their teams consistently to mission accomplishment are failing as leaders. We must accomplish the mission. If we are going to do so, we must first define it.

Part 1: Define It

How do we define our mission? The mission is our end state. It is where we want to go and what we want to achieve as an organization. The time period for that mission can be as short, or as long, as you need to accomplish it. A team could have a mission to win a particular game. A company could have a mission to reach a certain revenue level within a certain time period. Any and all personal and team actions taken during that time should be done to further mission accomplishment.

Some organizations use very narrow and clearly defined mission parameters. A football team may have a mission to win the national championship. Other organizations may avoid precise objective markers such as wins, points, or rankings and instead focus on a more subjective mission, such as reaching their true potential or creating an organization of which their community can be proud. Both approaches can work. What is most important is that everyone in the organization knows and understands the mission. It would be unfair to hold our subordinate leaders accountable to accomplishing the mission if we haven't clearly defined what it is. An effective mission always has a "why" attached to it. It is crucial that every member of the team know why they are doing what they are doing and what end they are working toward.

In the military we use "in order to" statements to explain our "why." For example, a unit could have a mission to capture an airfield "in order to" allow reinforcements to land. In Najaf, Mac and his fellow Marines knew that every action they undertook was done "in order to" bring peace to Najaf.

Part 2: Communicate It

One of the drills that we execute with teams and organizations during our experiential training involves a relay race of sorts. Some members of the team are running with sandbags while other are executing various exercises with a heavy log. There are various standards that the team must adhere to. For instance, as the sandbags are carried, they must stay together.

It is clearly explained to the leader that the mission is "as fast as possible." However, often when leaders brief their team, they leave out this crucial piece of information. They forget to tell their teammates what the mission is. Consequently, the first few times they try it, most of the team walks with the sandbags.

After a few slow and disastrous attempts, the Program instructor will ask some of the participants "What is the mission?" They will respond, "Keeping the sandbags together" or "Lifting the log." When we ask the leader, they respond, "As fast as possible." We then ask the rest of the team if they would have changed the way they attacked the drill knowing that the mission was "as fast as possible." Rather than walking with the sandbags, would they have sprinted with them? "Of course," they respond in the affirmative.

The mission must always be communicated down to the lowest level if we hope to accomplish it. It isn't enough if only half or even 80% of the team knows it. It is the leader's responsibility to ensure that every single team member knows and understands the mission.

It is the leader's responsibility to ensure that every single team member knows and understands the mission.

Part 3: Words on a Rock

Our mission should not be confused with a "mission statement." A corporate mission statement is often used to describe to potential customers the function, vision, and culture of the organization. A mission statement does not necessarily give the teammates and leaders of an organization an end state to work toward, or if it does, it is a very nebulous one. We joke with many athletic teams that somewhere on their campus, usually carved in stone, there is a long and beautifully written mission statement extolling the virtues and vision of the university. Not a single coach or athlete knows it (nor do any professors). Very few have ever even read it.

The mission of a team should be clear and concise so that it is understood by the entire team. Our mission, if our team is passionate about it, will help us make better decisions. We strive to take only those actions that further mission accomplishment and avoid actions that hamper it. We are willing to sacrifice for it. It is easy to do so when things are going well. Most importantly, we must also be able to do so in the most chaotic, confusing, and challenging environments in which we all battle. The decisions we make in those situations must advance us toward mission accomplishment, regardless of the adversity and uncertainly we face.

This is when a clear, concise, and actionable mission, that the entire team knows and supports, is most important.

Team leaders are held to two standards. First, they accomplish the mission. Following is how we do so.

29

The First Standard of a Leader: Accomplish the Mission

THE FIRST STANDARD to which a leader is held is Mission Accomplishment. The leader of an organization is responsible for everything that happens or fails to happen in that organization. Every Marine officer is taught this on the very first day of Officer Candidate School and it is reiterated and reinforced throughout their career.

The leader of an organization is responsible for everything that happens or fails to happen in that organization.

A few hours into the battle of Najaf, Mac and some of his Marines witnessed an American helicopter shot down. Najaf was the biggest fight in the entire area of operation at the time, so the Marines and sailors present received more support than ever before. It appeared that every type of aircraft in the U.S. arsenal was buzzing over their heads while dropping bombs and firing rockets into the cemetery. American helicopters were by far the most vulnerable aircraft to the enemy's return fire. They flew low and slow over the fighting, acquiring and engaging enemy targets, evacuating casualties, and providing intelligence to the ground forces. Mac's platoon was spread along a main road engaging enemy targets in the Najaf cemetery. Out of the corner of his eye, Mac saw a helicopter shudder and jerk. It swayed drunkenly over the ground, smoke belching out of a rear engine, and then it dropped. It didn't slam into the ground in an overly dramatic Hollywood fireball. Rather, it just dropped out of the sky like a puppet that had its strings cut. A plume of dust marked the crash site—in enemy-controlled territory.

Mac knew that enemy fighters would be racing for the helicopter and that the crew was in immediate danger.

"Who is closest to the crash site?" the Battalion Operations officer queried over the radio.

"This is Warpig. I've got it," Mac responded. Other units responded that they were in positions to support as well. Mac and his Marines were immediately tasked with rescuing the downed helicopter crew. It was their mission. It didn't matter that Mac and his Marines had been awake for over 35 hours and been in a serious life-or-death fire-fight for the last 5 hours. It didn't matter that some of Mac's best Marines had been seriously wounded and medically evacuated. It didn't matter that Mac had been shot in the shoulder an hour prior. The mission was to rescue the Marine helicopter crew, and Mac knew that accomplishing that mission was the standard to which he, as the leader of his unit, would be held.

He didn't have time to come up with a grandiose plan. Instead, he keyed the radio microphone on his helmet and said, "2 this is 1. On me. Go, go, go!" Sergeant Allen, Mac's point man, his "2," responded, "Roger," and they raced toward the crash site with their engines red-lined. They reached the helicopter at the same time as vehicles from a nearby Combined Anti-Armor Team (CAAT). Insurgents sprinted around the corner, guns raised, but the CAAT Marines and Marines from Mac's other vehicle shot them before they could reach the helicopter. The enemy concentrated their firepower on the area and bullets were cracking over the Marines' heads. Because the armor on Mac's LAVs was much stronger than the relatively thin skin of the helicopter, they positioned their vehicles between the helicopter and the enemy. Using the vehicles as cover from the enemy fire, Mac's scouts, along with Marines from the other units, were able to extract the helicopter crew. All were still alive. Mission accomplished.

Mac himself didn't shoot anyone, nor did he pull the pilots from the wreckage of their helicopter. However, along with his subordinate leaders, he made the decisions and provided the leadership that allowed his unit to accomplish their mission and saves the lives of three Marines.

As discussed in Section 1, the responsibility of command states that the leader gets more credit than deserved when the team does well. The leader also gets more blame than deserved when it doesn't. Great leaders distribute the former, but fully assume the latter.

This is a tough concept for some people to understand and may sound harsh. A Team Captain can play a tremendous game, can lead the team in scoring, and make head-turning plays. However, if the team's mission was to win the game and that didn't happen, the leader is responsible for that failure. A regional director of sales may be a wonderful human being, a great listener, emotionally intelligent, trustworthy, and great at sales. That person may even be responsible for closing the biggest sale in the region, but if the region's mission was to attain a certain revenue level and the region failed to do so, then he or she is failing as a leader.

In the military, Mac was counseled (putting it gently) more times than he cares to remember on mistakes that his Marines made. He wasn't the one who actually got behind the wheel after drinking. He wasn't actually the one who went into cold-weather training without packing warming layers, but he was still held responsible for these mistakes. Leaders are responsible for everything that happens or fails to happen in their units.

We are all willing to accept the benefits when the mission is accomplished. As leaders, we must be even more adamant about assuming the blame when it is not. If not, we can still be great athletes or salespeople, but we aren't leaders. Many have influence, but they aren't leaders. They may have an ability and they may even think they have the desire to be one, but an unwillingness or inability to accept the responsibility of command reflects otherwise.

President Truman kept a sign on his desk: "The buck stops here." The term originated during poker games in frontier days in which the dealer was marked by placing a Buck knife in front of him. If a player did not want the responsibility of dealing, he could "pass the Buck." President Truman understood that he was ultimately responsible for the governing of the country and that he could never pass it off. Too often this lesson is forgotten. We have all seen leaders who want the credit when things go well, but refuse to take responsibility for the failures of their organization. These kinds of leaders cannot build or sustain a championship culture.

How can we tell who they might be? Listen to them speak. Pronouns matter. Successes should be because "they [the team] did such a wonderful job." Mistakes should be because "I failed."

Leaders are responsible for everything that happens or fails to happen in their organization. Great leaders ensure consistent mission accomplishment.

30

Leaders Ask "How?"

THE FIRST STANDARD to which a leader is held accountable is to accomplish the mission. In the case of a corporate CEO or Head Coach of an athletic team, they (or their team) determine their mission. More often, as subordinate leaders, we are provided with one. In either case, we then must determine whom in our organization we task, and what those tasks should be (as well as how they "fit together"), for the successful accomplishment of that mission. The leader should involve subordinate leaders when doing so.

Involving our teammates allows the subject matter experts to give their valuable input. In the military, our greatest source of intelligence is provided by the troops "on the ground." Sometimes leaders are more involved with the battle at a "strategic" level rather than a "tactical" one, and they appreciate the input of those with more direct tactical involvement. On the athletic battlefield, players may be able to see certain tendencies or read an opponent's body language, information that is not readily available to their coach on the sideline. The same is true for corporate team leaders with their subordinate leaders and subject matter experts.

However, time, or the situation, may not afford the leader with the opportunity to ask subordinate leaders and teammates for advice or input. When the helicopter was shot down a few hours into the fight for Najaf, Mac didn't have time to ask his subordinate leaders for their thoughts and suggestions to rescue the downed helicopter crew. He simply commanded them to get "on him," and "Go. Go. Go."

As long as the senior leader has developed trust with teammates (accomplished in large part by their consistently accomplishing the second standard of a leader; more on this in the next chapter), the team will still strive for success and execute the plan at their 100%. They will be "all in." However, if time and the situation allow, the best and most successful leaders will involve their teammates in the planning process. As discussed in Section 1, asking for input from our "best" people in determining the team's standards provides ownership of the team to them. So, too, does soliciting their advice and input during the mission planning process.

"What is working?" University of Oregon Offensive Coordinator Scott Frost (now Nebraska head football coach) would ask his star quarterback, Marcus Mariotta, leading up to a game and during half-time. North Texas Head Coach Seth Littrell and Offensive Coordinator Graham Harrell (currently the Offensive Coordinator with the University of Southern California) would ask the same of their star quarterback, Mason Fine, as would Coach Josh Heupel with his own quarterback, McKenzie Milton. Vic Schaefer, the head coach of Mississippi State women's basketball, asked the same question of point guard Morgan William, as did John Tillman, Maryland men's lacrosse head coach, to midfielder Isaiah Davis-Allen. And they asked the question regardless of the score—whether the team was winning or losing.

These subordinate leaders have all earned that trust. Their coaches know that involving these subordinate leaders in the mission planning process will not only make for a stronger plan, but most importantly, also ensure that their subordinate leaders (and their teammates) commit to it and its execution at their 100%. It helps to ensure that they are also "all in." They are going to battle with ownership of the mission rather than just being handed a piece of paper and told to "get it done." The team views the mission, and the plan to successfully accomplish it, as their own. Ownership facilitates these feelings and beliefs. Further, regardless of the battlefield, as any leader will readily admit, a plan is very important, just not as much as it being executed with a violence of action. Ownership helps ensure it.

All great leaders ask for assistance from their subordinates in developing a plan to successfully accomplish the mission. Although these aforementioned coaches and players accomplish their missions very often, they don't always.

Although great leaders ask for input from subordinates, they *never* ask them to be responsible for it. Sometimes Marcus, Mason, or McKenzie throws an interception, Morgan turns the ball over, or Isaiah commits a costly penalty. On the even rarer occasions that their teams lose their battle, failing in the accomplishment of their mission, you will never hear their coach during the postgame press conference say, "Well, it was *their* idea." These coaches, military commanders, and all great leaders know that as *the* leader, they are ultimately responsible for everything that happens or fails to happen in their units. They— not their subordinate leaders whom they asked for assistance—are responsible for their team's mission accomplishment.

31

The Little Things Take Care of the Big Things

SOME LEADERS BELIEVE that their focus should only be on the "big things," and don't concern themselves with the "little things." We disagree. We have a saying in the Marines, "The *little* things take care of the *big* things." Mission accomplishment becomes nearly impossible if we lose focus of the details.

In the military, we have very specific rules and regulations as to how we wear our uniforms, how we cut our hair, and even how we lace our boots. That type of daily *attention to detail* may seem excessive, but we know that it is the details that often have life-or-death consequences. If we can't trust a young Marine to lace his boots left over right like he has been taught, we can't trust that Marine to call in an accurate grid of artillery when our position is being overrun by the enemy.

Simple details can have huge consequences. A football wide receiver breaking out of his route one yard too early or too late can be the difference between a game-winning touchdown and a game-ending drop. A defender in lacrosse not paying attention to her scouting report and knowing her opponent's tendencies can lead to her giving up a game-winning goal in overtime. A misplaced comma in a financial statement could lead to the loss of thousands or even millions of dollars.

Too often, leaders focus on these details only when mistakes have already been made and the consequences paid. The football coach, furious with his player for running the wrong route, says nothing when he walks into a filthy, cluttered, and disorganized locker room all week long upon completion of practice. The lacrosse coach may be upset with her defender for not paying attention to the scouting report, but never said anything all season when that same player showed up in an incorrect uniform. The director of finance was irate at the subordinate who made a mistake on the quarterly financial report, but consistently accepted emails and other correspondence from that same employee rife with typos and grammatical mistakes. The little things take care of the big things.

A few years ago, Mac attended the lacrosse game of one of our clients. Before and during the game, the coach consistently preached discipline and an attention to detail. Even as a non-lacrosse player, Mac could tell that the team played sloppy, disorganized, and undisciplined lacrosse. They made frequent mental mistakes and failed to recognize things that the coaches had clearly gone over in the scouting report in the locker room before the game. After the game, the coach asked Mac's thoughts. He told him that he was impressed with how hard his team fought, but that he wasn't surprised at the team's lack of discipline and attention to detail. As Mac said it, he gestured to the locker room around them. Each individual locker was an absolute mess. Clothes and sneakers lay haphazardly throughout the area. In the middle of the locker room there was a bin for players' dirty uniforms and towels. The players had just tossed their laundry in the general direction of the bin and sweaty jerseys and towels were strewn around it. Their locker room reflected their playing style. The little things take care of the big things.

The little things take care of the big things.

The Program is frequently invited to speak at conventions, clinics, and camps. At one of these clinics the speaker immediately preceding us was Eric Spoelstra, the head coach of the NBA's Miami Heat. Coach Spoelstra described a player he had coached who possessed an unmatched level of discipline and attention to detail. He recounted how this player's locker was almost OCD-like in its uniformity. His basketball shoes were always perfectly aligned on the floor, his jerseys neatly hung and color coordinated, and the deodorant was always in the same place. He went on to tell us that that player was LeBron James, one of the greatest players of all time. He appreciates that a fanatical devotion to discipline and an attention to detail is what will make him truly great. The little things take care of the big things.

If we want to ensure a detail-focused, organized, and disciplined team on a *particular* battlefield, we must ensure they are detail-focused, organized, and disciplined on *every* battlefield. As leaders, we must focus on the details both in our own personal lives and in our organizations. If we allow our teammates to demonstrate a poor attention to detail during the daily performance of their duties, and we fail to hold them accountable, we can blame only ourselves when our organization demonstrates poor attention to detail on game day, regardless of the playing field.

Here are some outward signs of a detail-oriented team:

1. Clean and organized common areas
2. Dress code
3. Well groomed (even if you just rolled out of bed, you don't *look* like you did)
4. Punctual
5. Gear and equipment treated as if you bought it
6. Notepad and pen for all meetings

Action Items on Accomplishing the Mission

1. Ensure that you, as the leader, know your team's mission and have communicated it to the entire organization. If not, do so immediately!
2. If time and the situation allows, solicit advice from subordinate leaders on how to accomplish your organization's mission.
3. Be aware of the big picture, but stay focused (and ensure your team stays focused) on the "mission critical" details that will help the team accomplish the mission.

Saved Round on Accomplishing the Mission

Leaders accomplish the mission. To assist in their doing so, remember the leadership lesson that Mac (and all Marine Corps officers) are taught early and reinforced throughout their careers: "Don't ever ask your Marines to do something that you are not willing to do yourself." If you do so, it will undermine trust.

The Program founder, Eric Kapitulik's, seven-year-old son, Axel, participates on a "Youth Ninja Team" at a facility called Ultimate Obstacles in West Boylston, Massachusetts. His coach is excellent and he (and Eric) continuously challenge Axel to push himself outside his comfort zone on all the obstacles (imagine American Ninja Warrior obstacles for kids). When Axel first started, he was incapable of completing the monkey bars. After three months of physical and mental toughness, hard work, and not making excuses (all of which we will discuss in the following sections), Axel does them with ease.

Despite an incredibly intense schedule while traveling, The Program team still *makes* the time to work out. On one business trip, Eric finished his workout at almost ten o'clock at night. The gym had a set of monkey bars. Eric was leaving the gym exhausted from two days of travel, working with an important corporate client, and the workout he had just completed. He glanced at the gym's monkey bars and continued to the locker room. While showering, though, he couldn't stop thinking about those darn monkey bars. He didn't want to do them, he was tired, he didn't feel good—all the same excuses his son gives his coach (or Eric) prior to trying new things that they ask (read "force") him to do.

In any event, Eric got out of the shower, put his sweaty workout clothes back on, and did the monkey bars. As leaders, we must all remember to do the same with whatever the monkey bars are in our own organizations. As a team, we may determine that our co-workers arriving five minutes early for a meeting with a pen and notebook will help our team accomplish its mission. We demand that they do so. We must ensure that we do the same.

Unfortunately, we don't, and it undermines trust within our organization. Peers and subordinates don't trust that we will also do the things we are expecting of them. Trust is the foundation of every relationship. A lack of trust is indicative of a lack of team cohesion, which obviously imperils its ability to accomplish the mission.

Thankfully, the opposite is also true. If we ask our teammates to eat their vegetables and they see us eating them too, they may not enjoy them any more than Axel initially enjoyed the monkey bars, but they *trust* that we aren't asking them to do something that we aren't also willing to do. Greater trust produces a corresponding increase in team cohesion and its ability to accomplish the mission, the first standard to which we are held. We will now discuss the second.

32

The Second Standard of a Leader: Take Care of Your Teammates

THE SECOND STANDARD to which every leader is held is Take Care of Your Teammates. When Eric was at the Infantry Officer's Course (IOC), he and his teammates had an opportunity to meet a Marine Corps legend. They were coming to the tail end of "The War," the culminating exercise at IOC, and a brutal test of their leadership ability while battling hunger, extreme fatigue, and brutal weather conditions. There was over two feet of snow on the ground for its entirety. Eric and his teammates knew someone important was arriving when they were called in and ordered to sit around a large fire to prepare for the guest speaker. It was the first warmth they had been allowed in almost two weeks, and they knew that it had to be quite a special guest. They were still surprised when they were joined by General Al Gray. General Gray had served as the 29th Commandant in the Marine Corps and was revered as a leader and a warrior. For his official commandant's picture, he chose not to wear the dress blue uniform (the Marine Corps' formal uniform adorned with medals and ribbons) that every commandant before, and since, has worn. Instead, he took the photo wearing his camouflage uniform, the uniform that Marines wear into battle.

As infantry officers in training, the opportunity to spend time with Al Gray was special. The young lieutenants were afforded the opportunity to ask him questions about his experiences. One of the lieutenants asked for the best piece of advice he could give that would ensure their being successful as Marine officers. Without hesitation, General Gray started by explaining that "being successful" meant a lot of different things to different people, just as it would for the young lieutenants surrounding the fire that night. He went on to clarify that to some, being successful might mean becoming a general or, even more impressive, attaining the title of commandant. Having accomplished both, he didn't define "being successful" that way and he suggested that the young infantry officers didn't either. As he highlighted, the title you achieve in every organization other than your family is more of a reflection of your reputation. Reputation is what *other* people think you are. Instead, be more focused on your character. Character is who you actually are.

General Gray went on to further explain that he wasn't sure if those in attendance that day would serve in the Marine Corps for 4 years or, like him, for 41 years. Therefore, rather than provide guidance on how to be successful as a Marine Corps officer, he wanted to share with them how to be a "success" throughout their entire life, not just the period of it that they would spend on active duty. General Gray proceeded to tell the Marines, "Warriors, as the term would suggest, to be successful, you must accomplish the mission. Whatever your mission is as an individual and more importantly on the teams of which you will be privileged to be a part, do so honorably, but accomplish it." General Gray continued, "But to be a true 'success,' you must take care of your people, be they your Marines, your corporate co-workers, and most certainly, your friends and family. Your children do not have the luxury of choosing their parents. You, however, will have a choice as to what sort of father you will be. This will be generally true for you throughout your entire life on all the teams of which you will be a part. Your subordinates don't choose you, but you will have a choice of what type of leader you will be *for* them. Therefore, to be a success, accomplish the mission and take care of your teammates. The way you do so is by making every single decision you ever make by thinking about what is in the best interest of the team, first!" General Gray, a no-nonsense, straight-shooter communicator, closed this way: "I guarantee you that not all of you will." He paused. "Titles, money, your reputation, who other people think you are, will become a greater priority than those two standards that I spoke of that help ensure the success of the teams you will lead throughout your life."

As someone who has no problem with silence, General Gray finished and just sat there staring at the young lieutenants. None moved. Only a few even breathed. After what seemed like an eternity, Eric's best friend, Naval Academy and IOC classmate, and fellow infantry officer Doug Zembiec, the toughest of all the lieutenants, stood up, screamed "WOOOOOHOOOOOOO!" at the absolute maximum volume, in the middle of the Virginia wilderness, and started clapping and cheering wildly.

Anyone who knew or served with Doug Zembiec (KIA May 11, 2007, Baghdad, Iraq), one of the biggest successes and most legendary Marines in modern times, will attest that he did accomplish the mission and he did take care of his people. Every single decision he ever made was done with his team's best interest at heart first. For those other Marines who also shared the fire that day, they will also attest that not all of them did.

We all define "being successful" differently, but by The Program's definition, like General Gray's, the most successful leaders on any battlefield consistently accomplish the mission and take care of their people. Not all leaders do, though. As General Gray highlighted, titles, money, our reputation, and who other people think we are, all become a greater priority than those two standards. Don't allow it. Stay focused on accomplishing the mission and making every decision we make with the team's best interest at heart first. Take care of your people.

33

Mission First, People Always

ALL LEADERS ARE held to two standards: accomplish the mission and take care of your people. Taking care of your people is easy. As young Marine Corps officers, we certainly thought so. We enjoyed taking care of our Marines. We were good at it. Initially, "taking care of our Marines" meant letting them out early on a Friday, it meant getting some "hot wets" (hot coffee and soup) brought out to the field when we were training in the cold. Taking care of our Marines, our "people," meant making popular decisions that helped our Marines like us. We would come to realize just how wrong we were.

Jake MacDonald and his platoon were one of the first conventional units to cross the border during the invasion of Iraq in 2003. It is tough to adequately put into words the chaos and stress they were feeling at the time. Mac's unit had been tasked with patrolling the Kuwaiti side of the border in the days leading up to the invasion. When everything kicked off on the night of March 19, they had already been awake and working for close to 24 hours. They crossed the border into Iraq at night. The oil fields had been set ablaze and they could barely see through all the smoke. Due to the threat of weapons of mass destruction, they wore full chemical suits, and every time they took incoming enemy fire, they had to put on gas masks, often for hours at a time. Their greatest advantages on the battlefield were speed and violence of action, so there was no time to stop. No time to rest, eat, or drink. This was the first time in combat for Mac and his Marines and they fully expected to run into a battalion of enemy tanks every time they crested a rise or turned a corner. The constant ebb and flow of adrenaline only added to their fatigue.

After moving for another 24 hours (a total of 48), they were finally given the order to stop and set into a security position. Mac knew that he would finally be getting a chance to get some sleep and food. He knew his Marines would get the same, and the overall feeling of pleasure was palpable.

However, as soon as they had moved their vehicles into position, Mac's commanding officer, Captain (at the time) Gil Juarez, requested that Mac and the other leaders rendezvous at his own vehicle. When Mac arrived, the first thing Captain Juarez said had nothing to do with his personal welfare. He did not ask, "How are you?" Instead, he said, "Mac, I need a patrol out within the next 10 minutes." Mac answered, "Yes, sir," but inside he was seething. Didn't the boss know how tired and hungry Mac and his platoon were? Didn't he know how to take care of his Marines?

Mac continued to rage internally at the unfairness of it all on the walk back to his platoon. However, as Mac admits, by the time he got there, he was embarrassed. He realized that taking care of his Marines was exactly what his commanding officer was doing!

As General Gray taught, at The Program, we define taking care of our people as "*making every decision we ever make with the team's best interests at heart.*" Captain Juarez knew exactly how tired and hungry Mac's platoon was. He hadn't slept or eaten either. He knew how badly the entire company wanted sleep and how much they would resent an order to immediately *go back out*. However, he also knew that taking care of Mac and all his Marines had nothing to do with being nice to them. It had nothing to do with sleep, food, or comfort. In that situation, it meant making sure Marines were outside of the lines, watchful and aware to ensure no bad guys attacked their sleeping teammates. Taking care of his Marines meant bringing all of them home alive to their loved ones, and he was willing to make unpopular decisions in order to make sure he brought those Marines home.

At The Program, we define taking care of people as "making every decision with the team's best interests at heart."

Making every decision with the team's best interests at heart rarely means giving the answer the team might want to hear. It involves holding your teammates accountable to the standards of your organization. It may mean taking the keys of a teammate who's been drinking, knocking on a door to make sure a teammate gets to an early class, or correcting a teammate whose behavior is hurting mission accomplishment. These actions may not make you more popular or better liked. You do them because you care about the well-being of your teammates and are willing to make unpopular decisions because they are in the best interests of your teammates and, most importantly, the entire team.

The team accomplishing its mission is in the best interests of its teammates. We stay focused on the mission first, but on our teammates always. "Taking care of our teammates" means making every decision not with wants and desires as the priority, but with the team's best *interests* at heart.

34

Controlled and Uncontrolled Environments

IN ORDER TO take care of our teammates we must ensure that they can succeed in the confusion and chaos of competition. As stated in the previous chapter, taking care of your teammates does not necessarily mean making sure they are comfortable and always having fun. In the Marine Corps it meant demanding our teammates did everything necessary to ensure that they would arrive home alive to their loved ones after accomplishing our mission. It means making sure your teammates are truly prepared for their competition so that they can accomplish the mission and reap the rewards for doing so.

There are two clearly delineated types of environments: controlled and uncontrolled. A *controlled environment* is one where we control the variables: we choose the location, duration, and intensity level of any training. An example would be practice, or the weight room, for most athletic teams. For corporate America, examples include a simulated cold-call training session with sales staff, or simply a "normal" business day.

In an *uncontrolled environment*, there is an enemy out there trying to kill us, figuratively (athletic or corporate) or literally (military combat operations; police, fire, and other emergency first responders). For corporate America, we can think of an uncontrolled environment as any "normal" day that becomes abnormal: our biggest client unexpectedly leaves us, our firm lays off 10% of its workforce, or we are rushing to meet a tight deadline.

In training and practice, leaders should make their controlled environments seem uncontrolled. We should try to replicate game-time or battlefield conditions: do a "two-minute drill", but give the offense one minute to do it in; tell participants that their simulated cold calls will each last five minutes and then make them three. Even though we can never truly replicate the stress of an actual uncontrolled environment, we must add adversity to our controlled environments to help the team prepare for them.

By the same token, *leaders must make uncontrolled environments appear as controlled as possible.* Many don't. Leaders may not be responsible for "the fire," but there is no need to add fuel to it. Unfortunately, many leaders make uncontrolled environments appear even more out of control. Behind in a game, coaches yell, scream, and smash clipboards. Business leaders get just as emotional and make already tense, challenging meetings, or days, even more so.

Instead, even if you don't feel cool, calm, and in control, communicate and act as if you do (more on communication in Section 7), which gives confidence to your team. Leadership is influence. If a leader "loses their cool," that influences subordinates and they will lose theirs.

Making controlled environments appear as uncontrolled as possible, and then ensuring that we do the opposite while in uncontrolled ones, is *taking care of our teammates.* It allows them to focus on the mission in front of them instead of the fear within them. In the military, it allows Mac to bring his Marines home from Iraq. In business, we are able to provide more products and better services to our clients. This allows us to reach our sales targets, which leads to increased salaries and bonuses (and all of our teammates will agree that that *is* in their best interest).

Improving your performance through controlled and uncontrolled environments

1. Here are some suggestions to make your controlled (practice/training) environments seem uncontrolled:
   a. Find ways to add stress to the environment. If your environment is physical, find ways to fatigue your team before executing normal drills. Use loud music or noise to cause distraction.

b. Use fear of the unknown. Do not tell your team exactly what they will be doing or how long they will be doing it.

c. Find other job- or sports-specific ways to present some chaos. Shorten the play clock. Simulate an injury and replace one of the usual participants. Change the scenario at the last second.

2. Here are some suggestions to make your uncontrolled (game time/ field of battle) environments seem controlled:

a. Use the same drills, procedures, and rituals that you do during training.

b. Lower the pitch and volume of your voice to take any panic out of it.

c. Give your team all the information they need to be successful, but no more than that.

Action Items for Taking Care of Your Teammates

1. Before every decision you ever make in your organization, ask yourself these two questions:

a. Will this decision bring our organization closer to accomplishing the mission? If the answer is no, don't do it. If the answer is yes, execute.

b. Is this decision in the best interests of my team and teammates (not my own)? If the answer is no, don't do it. If the answer is yes, execute.

2. As the leader, make every decision with your team's best interest at heart. Unfortunately, this may not be a popular decision or one that will make you more well-liked.

3. To increase your odds of mission accomplishment on any battlefield, make your controlled environments appear uncontrolled, and your uncontrolled environments appear controlled.

Saved Round on Taking Care of Your Teammates

For the leaders of successful, well-balanced organizations, accomplishing their mission and taking care of their people is often one and the same. Making every decision with the best interests of their team at heart is the best way to ensure mission success. This holds true for military organizations as well. However, sometimes in combat it seems like mission accomplishment and taking care of your people are leagues apart.

Early in the Battle of Najaf, as he and his platoon were in their own firefight, Mac listened in horror as one of the other officers in the unit called in an Urgent Surgical Casualty Evacuation (the most serious kind) on Mac's best friend, Dave Lewis. Mac had known Dave for years and they had been roommates in Southern California for the last two. Dave was leading his infantry platoon through a brutal period of fighting. As he knelt next to a crypt in the cemetery where they were fighting, Dave saw a flash of light in the corner of his eye. He glanced up to see a rocket-propelled grenade streaking toward him. Dave barely had enough time to duck his head before the rocket struck. Amazingly, instead of exploding immediately, the rocket hit his Kevlar helmet and bounced a few feet in the air before detonating. Although it didn't kill him straight out, the blast knocked him out, and the shrapnel tore apart his face and upper torso. When Dave awoke, he had been completely blinded, yet his own Marines had to hold him down to stop him from attempting to rejoin the firefight with his blood quickly pooling around him.

At the time, Mac knew none of this. He knew only that an urgent evacuation had been called. The officer who called it in was hesitant to use Dave's name because he didn't want to damage the morale of the other Marines by notifying them that one of their most beloved leaders was down. However, after repeated requests for his identity, the reporting officer used Dave's callsign, "Blackhorse 2," to inform Mac that his best friend was injured and quite possibly dying.

(continued)

Saved Round on Taking Care of Your Teammates (Cont'd)

Naturally, Mac wanted desperately to drop what he was doing and rush to his injured friend's side. Instead, he muttered a quick prayer for Dave and got back in his own firefight. That may sound callous to an outside observer, but combat simplifies many things into their black-and-white essence. Mac had a mission to accomplish. He knew that if he abandoned that mission to go to his friend, other Marines could be injured or killed. Furthermore, Mac had thirty other Marines who were looking to him for leadership and guidance in the middle of their own brutal fight. Dave would have done exactly the same thing if the roles were reversed. Leaders must accomplish the mission, and running to Dave's aid would have hurt Mac's own unit's ability to do so. It would not have been taking care of his people, because it would have been counter to the best interests of his unit.[1]

Leaders are held to two standards: accomplish the mission and take care of your teammates. Every decision we ever make is done with the best interests of our team at heart. The best interests of our team and teammates is ensuring that we stay focused on accomplishing the mission. If not, in the military, many more people are killed in the long run. In our own daily lives, many more people's livelihoods are destroyed.

Leaders who constantly prioritize their own personal interests and desires or those of individuals on the team, before accomplishing the mission, inevitably hurt many more on the team. If the mission is to reach a particular revenue amount and we don't reach it, then the consequence can be layoffs to numerous members of the team, or even the whole business filing for bankruptcy. The first scenario negatively affects those who are, and even those members of the team who aren't, losing their job. They will have

---

[1] Dave Lewis was medevaced to Germany and then Bethesda Naval Hospital, where he remained blind for more than 6 months. After numerous surgeries, he regained sight in one eye. He continues to remove shrapnel from the left side of his body. In 2012, Mac and Dave were best men at each other's weddings.

to assume more work and greater responsibility at no extra salary (a business can't increase salaries if it doesn't have the money to pay them). This also doesn't consider the physical, mental, and emotional toll that layoffs cause to everyone in an organization.

Furthermore, individuals who consistently ask a leader to put personal needs first are in effect saying that an individual's needs are more important than the team's. They are not, and leaders who allow this are failing in their role.

Now that we have established what leadership is and isn't, who leaders are and aren't, and have defined the standards to which leaders are held, we address the biggest question The Program receives (and is hired to address): How do you develop them?

35

Developing Leaders

TEACHING LEADERSHIP IS one thing, and for the most part, teams who hire
The Program already do a decent job of it. Developing leadership is
another matter.

Down by 17 at half-time, the coach gives a screaming, profanity-laced
speech. Red-faced and with spittle flying, he grabs his star player and
yells, "I need you to be a better leader." After seeing her three-year
team captain graduate, the coach calls one of her incoming seniors
into her office and says, "Now it is your turn. I need you to lead." A
managing director or regional sales manager unexpectedly departs a
firm. The CEO tells the next most senior person or best salesperson
that they are now the new leader of that branch or region.

In all these scenarios, those athletes or individuals are set up for
failure. Teaching leadership makes people aware of what good leaders
(and bad) do. Unfortunately, it doesn't make you one. To become a
leader, we must be developed. In order to do so with the future leaders
within your organization (family, athletic team, corporation, school,
etc.), leaders must take—or more probably, *find*—opportunities to provide subordinates with three things:

1. A task they are to accomplish
2. Conditions under or with which they must work
3. A standard to which it must be completed

Nearly everything we do in the Marine Corps has a task, condition, and standard associated with it, from making your rack (bed) at boot camp to engaging a moving target with an M40A4 sniper rifle. We constantly put young leaders in charge of smaller tasks, and then hold them accountable for the results. We do this so that the first time they must lead isn't when they are unexpectedly thrust into the role during a combat patrol in Marjah, Afghanistan.

Leadership Means Accountability

An easy example of where this process can be applied for leaders of athletic teams is the locker room. Messy locker rooms drive coaches crazy. How we do small things is how we do all things. If we are going to be disciplined on the field, it needs to start in the locker room. However, this can be difficult for an 18-year-old (or a 44- or 64-year-old) to grasp. As discussed earlier, the head coach must stay focused on the details, but that is not to say that they must be the person who is responsible for the cleanliness of the locker room. Instead, assign one athlete who has influence, as well as the desire and ability to be a leader, to be in charge of the locker room. Better tasks for subordinates' leadership development are those that entail them working with and influencing other co-workers. That person's "task" is to ensure the cleanliness of the locker room, and the "conditions" include the cleaning supplies available and the help of teammates. Set up one locker that looks the way you want them all to look. This is "the standard." Explain to the student-athlete leader that all lockers must look identical to this one and that they will be held accountable for the results.

The next time you, the coach, walk into the locker room and see a towel on the ground, you don't lose your mind on the team. You don't even yell at the athlete who threw the towel on the ground. Instead, you call into your office the student-athlete whom you assigned as leader and who accepted the responsibility of the locker room's cleanliness, and you hold that person accountable. Hopefully, that athlete will improve communication and accountability with teammates. You can offer to help with this. If the person complains that it isn't fair to be held accountable for someone else leaving a towel on the floor, that communicates either a lack of understanding that leaders are responsible for the performance and actions of others (and it needs to be explained), or that the person simply doesn't want to be a true leader. As discussed earlier in this section, a leader needs influence and both the desire and the ability to be one. Although still challenging, ability can be developed more easily than desire.

On most athletic teams, however, team captains are allowed to call themselves "leaders" merely for calling "heads or tails" prior to a game. If you are not responsible and held accountable for the performance of anyone else on your team, you are not a leader of it. In corporate America, leaders must simply assign greater responsibility (a task) to their subordinates. If there is anything (conditions) that can help them (and their teammates) to accomplish this, communicate it to them, along with your expectations (standards) for its successful accomplishment. Then hold that individual accountable. Remember that to best develop a subordinate's leadership ability, assign a task that entails them working with and influencing other co-workers. If the task doesn't involve these two things, you are not developing your subordinate's leadership—you are just giving them more work.

Start with Small Responsibilities

Certain things are critical to mission accomplishment, and the leaders or their immediate subordinates must stay responsible for them. Delegate everything else to those whose leadership you wish to develop. The challenge initially is that they won't be as efficient or effective as you or your immediate subordinates. Manage your own expectations and remember that, initially, you weren't as efficient or effective as the guy who came before you either.

When we work with teams, at the conclusion of the first day of training, we select one participant and tell them everything they need to know for the following morning's training. It is then their responsibility to communicate that information to everyone else on the team and ensure that they show up on time and in the proper uniform. This can make coaches or business leaders very uncomfortable. Many would rather tell the team themselves or put an assistant in charge. We look at it differently: if someone shows up five minutes late the next morning or in the wrong uniform, we will still have a great day of training, and by holding the individual accountable whom we put in charge, they will learn a valuable leadership lesson.

Leaders get held accountable to two standards: accomplish the mission, and take care of your people. Giving young leaders a task, condition, and standard is a great way to develop them. If you expect your subordinates to lead, don't let the fourth quarter, a big project, or a combat patrol be the first time they have done so.

If you expect your subordinates to lead, don't let the fourth quarter, a big project, or a combat patrol be the first time they have done so.

The Process of Developing Leaders

1. Select some upcoming leaders whom you want to develop.
2. Assign them a task to accomplish and explain the conditions they must work under and the standard to which the task is to be completed.
3. Hold those teammates personally accountable for the results.
4. As they develop as leaders, give them increased responsibility and more challenging tasks.

36

The Power of Delegation

MOST LEADERS HAVE earned their position through outstanding performance. Typically, in corporate America, a region's best salesperson is named regional sales director when that position opens. In college football, the best offensive, defensive, and special team coordinators are promoted to head coach. However, the things that make a subordinate leader great can hurt that individual when they are promoted to the top position if they are unable to adapt to the new role.

Typically, great subordinate leaders want their leader to give them as much ownership over various parts of the organization as possible. Their subsequent great performance in those areas is what allows them to be promoted in the first place.

A great salesperson typically makes the most sales calls to clients and prospects, and in doing so helps the team to be successful. However, as regional sales director, if the person is still spending their time that way, it has exactly the opposite effect on the team's success. For the sales team to be most effective, the regional sales director must stay focused on the things that only he or she can do: training the sales people, attending meetings with the biggest clients and prospects, determining compensation, and so on.

Similarly, there are certain things that only a head coach can do. For example, it is great to have an assistant coach sit down and talk to recruits and their parents inside their homes. However, it just isn't the same as when the head coach walks in and does this. Both coaches are *saying* that the school wants that recruit to play for them, but the latter scenario *shows* it.

For a head coach to have the time that it takes to be in that living room, or a regional sales director to effectively counsel all of the salespeople in their region, they must delegate ownership of other tasks to their subordinates. If they do not, the organization will not function as efficiently as it could, and performance will suffer. Those coaches or business leaders will then find themselves on the "hot seat."

The best leaders are those that stay solely focused on only those things that the leader can and must do for the organization to be successful. Everything else is delegated to subordinate leaders. While the leader ultimately remains responsible for everything that happens or fails to happen in the organization, in the most successful organizations, the leaders have delegated everything possible to their subordinates, other than that which only they can do.

If they are unable or unwilling to do so, the first step is the hot seat. The next is no seat.

37

Leadership Is a Contact Sport

Figure 37.1 Mortar rounds exploding near Captain John Ripley at Dongha.
Note: Image courtesy of U.S. Naval Museum and with appreciation to Tom and Steve Ripley.

Colonel John Ripley, Navy Cross Citation:
The Navy Cross is awarded to Captain John W. Ripley, United States Marine Corps, for extraordinary heroism on 2 April 1972 while serving as the Senior Marine Advisor to the Third Vietnamese Marine Corps Infantry Battalion in the Republic of Vietnam. Upon receipt of a report that a rapidly moving, mechanized, North Vietnamese army force, estimated at reinforced divisional strength, was attacking south along Route #1, the Third Vietnamese Marine Infantry Battalion was positioned to defend a key village and the surrounding area. It became imperative that a vital river bridge be destroyed if the overall security of the northern provinces of Military Region One was to be maintained. Advancing to the bridge to personally supervise this most dangerous, but vitally important assignment, Captain Ripley located a large amount of explosives which had been prepositioned there earlier, access to which was blocked by a chain-link fence. In order to reposition the approximately 500 pounds of explosives, Captain Ripley was obliged to reach up and hand-walk along the beams while his body dangled beneath the bridge. On five separate occasions, in the face of constant enemy fire, he moved to points along the bridge and, with the aid of another advisor who pushed the explosives to him, securely emplaced them. He then detonated the charges and destroyed the bridge, thereby stopping the enemy assault. By his heroic actions and extraordinary courage, Captain Ripley undoubtedly was instrumental in saving an untold number of lives. His inspiring efforts reflected great credit upon himself, the Marine Corps, and the United States Naval Service.[1]

Eric Kapitulik met Colonel Ripley while a midshipman and member of the varsity lacrosse team at the United States Naval Academy. Colonel Ripley was a sports enthusiast and loved lacrosse in particular (although he may have told this to every team on campus). In any event, they became good friends, especially when Eric returned to the Naval Academy as a Marine Corps officer. His best friend, also a Marine Corps officer, Doug Zembiec (KIA Iraq 2007) and Eric had

---

[1] Navy Department Board of Decorations and Medals

the privilege of spending countless hours with Colonel Ripley, prior to his death in 2008. (It was Colonel Ripley who called Eric to tell him that his best friend had died in 2007.) Every interaction with Colonel Ripley was a lesson on leadership.

However, the one that Eric and The Program team is constantly reminded of is *"Leadership is a contact sport."* Leadership requires us to be present and to interact with our teammates. "Let's go guys," has never actually made anyone "go."

"Let's go guys" has never actually made anyone "go."

Question: How often do we see a quarterback come to the sideline after a three-and-out series, get on the headset with his offensive coordinator, take a sip of water, and then continue to sit in that same spot until it is his turn to get back on the field?

Answer: As often as a manufacturing shift manager sits in his or her office for an entire eight-hour shift "managing," while their teammates are on the floor of the plant working. As often as a principal or mayor sits in his or her office doing paperwork for an entire day, while the teachers or fellow government workers are in their own separate rooms or offices.

Instead, as the quarterback, come to the sideline, talk to your coach, get a sip of water, and then walk up the sideline. Pat your teammates on the back. Hug 'em! Managers, leave your cell phone in your office (the paperwork and emails will always be there), walk around the plant or office floor, shake hands, pat people on the back, and communicate with your corporate teammates, fellow teachers, and government employee teammates. Remember Colonel Ripley: "Leadership is a contact sport."

There are a host of reasons why we may not be able to constantly shake hands and pat backs. We must also successfully complete all of the tasks associated with our job's title for our team to successfully accomplish its mission. Sometimes the quarterback does need to speak with the offensive coordinator for an entire opponent's possession. Sometimes a corporate manager has personnel "fires" that must be addressed or deadlines that may preclude them from doing so. Marketing managers must market and manage. A director of sales must direct sales. However, regardless of the battlefield, as a leader (someone who has influence and has an ability and desire to use it), if at any time you are frustrated, angry, upset, or worried, if you are facing adversity and feel the corresponding stress associated with it, know that your team has those same feelings. In those moments, we must remember that that is when our teams need our influence, that is when we must remember "Leadership is a contact sport." It is how we maximize our influence and ensure our team's ultimate success.

The Program has the privilege of working with more than 150 athletic and corporate teams annually. These teams range in size from very small to having a worldwide footprint; they may be entirely located in a one-room office or have hundreds of offices around the world. There are indeed factors that make it more challenging for leadership to be a contact sport. More challenging, but not impossible.

Impossible is blowing up a steel bridge with 500 pounds of explosives, while the enemy shoots at you and you climb hand over hand placing the explosives. Colonel Ripley blew up the bridge. We can shake our teammates' hands. Leadership is a contact sport.

38

The Roles of a Leader

THE STANDARDS OF a leader are different from the roles of a leader. Please don't confuse the two. Leaders are held to two standards: accomplish the mission and take care of your teammates. All leaders will more effectively be able to achieve those *standards* if they understand and can assume the three *roles* of a leader: commander, coach, and mentor.[1]

Mentoring is about building a culture and teaching our teammates what it means to be "one of us." Coaching, in our vernacular, is teaching our teammates the skills they need to succeed—the X's and O's of how we do things. This could be blocking and tackling in football, sales techniques and procedures in the corporate world, or shooting and close-combat techniques in the military. Commanding is the act of giving direct orders.

Initially, we visualize these roles as a pyramid, as shown in Figure 38.1, for two reasons. One, as a ratio of time, it takes much longer to mentor someone than it does to coach them, and more time to coach than to command. Mentoring can, and often does, last a lifetime. Coaching is an ongoing process, but athletic coaches at every level have rules that outline how much time they can spend on X's and O's with their players. Corporate America does not impose this time limitation on training, but we have numerous responsibilities in our

---

[1] This is something that a former teammate brought to us, but we are unsure of who that teammate was and of the origins of the "three roles of a leader."

134

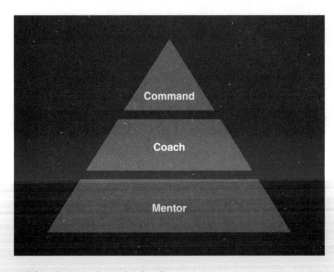

Figure 38.1 The three roles of a leader.

lives and therefore there are systemic limitations on how much time we can spend doing so. Commanding takes very little time. It could be as simple as "John, shift left" during a basketball game, a "frag order" in the military (i.e., "2 this is 1. On me. Go, go, go!"), or giving very pointed directions to a corporate teammate.

Second, the pyramid also represents the structure of an effective organization and how its leaders fulfill their roles. The foundation of any organization is its culture, what it means to be "one of us." We can coach our teammates on the skills they need to succeed, and we can command them, but if we have not mentored them on what it means to be "one of us"—if they don't fit our culture—they will fail, and so will we as an organization. Commanding is also very counterproductive if we have not first coached our teammates on the skills and procedures of how we do what we do to be successful. Therefore, especially initially, much more time should be spent mentoring than coaching, and more time coaching than commanding.

Part 1: Building Esprit de Corps

The military uses this pyramid very effectively. First, young soldiers, airmen, sailors, and Marines are sent to basic training or boot camp.

There is a significant amount of yelling at boot camp. It is used to make young recruits uncomfortable. Much more time and effort is spent with young men and women mentoring them throughout, and an esprit de corps, a common warrior spirit, is created. This mentoring process continues throughout their career.

Graduates of enlisted boot camp or officer training have little to no understanding of tactics or basic warfare. However, after graduating, they are sent to their military job-specific school (infantry school, communication school, logistics school, etc.). Furthermore, after this entry-level training, coaching continues throughout a military member's career on the skills they will need to succeed in their designated role. Finally, once we are "in the fight," we can effectively command each other.

Too often we see organizations with their pyramid unintentionally upside down. The senior leaders spend all their time commanding and little time mentoring. This occurs most often with new members to the organization, whether they're freshman basketball players or new members of a marketing team. "Hey freshman, pick up the balls after practice." Or "Hey, new person, set up the presentation room." Those new teammates will benefit far more from mentoring than will anyone else. It is of little to no value commanding them if we have not already mentored them into "one of us."

Part 2: Intentionally Inverting the Pyramid

However, sometimes it is indeed necessary to invert the pyramid (see Figure 38.2). We believe firmly that if we recruit someone to our organization, we owe it to them to mentor them. However, as discussed in Section 1, there are times when we invest our resources (time and money) mentoring someone on what it means to be "one of us" and we get no return on that investment. We truly believe we can change that individual and so we continue to mentor them while we continue to receive little or no positive return on that time investment. We never want to give up on someone, so we continue to mentor them even though we see no positive change or improvement. At some point, we realize we have poured years of time and effort into mentoring this individual (who, not coincidentally, is usually talented) and yet they will never fit our culture. Meanwhile, we have members of our organization

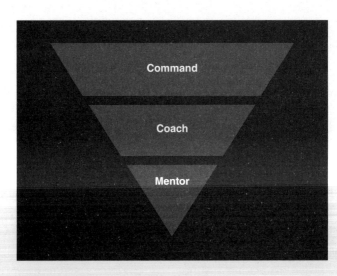

Figure 38.2 Inverting the pyramid.

who could greatly benefit from our mentoring, but we don't give it to them because we're spending all our time and effort trying to mentor and change someone who will never be "one of us."

There comes a point, and this is the "art" side of leadership, where we need to invert the pyramid. There is no precise time to do so, but eventually we must decide to spend the majority of our time commanding them. We are still going to spend the same amount of time "coaching" them, but instead of spending all our valuable time trying to change someone who is choosing not to do so, we are just going to command them; to tell them where to go and what to do. Finally, after we flip the triangle, if the individual still does not change their behavior, the only next step is for that individual to leave the organization.

We cannot tell you when to flip the triangle on someone, but whenever one of our clients has followed our recommendation to do so, the common feedback is, "Wow, I should have done that months ago." Many leaders will push back on this and say that they never want to give up on a teammate. Our response is that leaders are held to two standards: accomplish the mission and take care of our teammates. We do so by making every decision by thinking of what is in the best interests of the team, first and foremost, not what's best for any one individual, and certainly not for any individual who provides no return on the leader's investment of time. Our allegiance isn't to the individual; it is to the team.

Our allegiance isn't to the individual; it is to the team.

Inverting the pyramid does not mean giving up on a teammate. We are still going to coach that person to the best of our ability. We will just spend more time commanding and less time mentoring that teammate to ensure that we will still accomplish our mission and take care of *all* our people. We realize that our loyalty is not to a specific person, but to the unit as a whole. As soon as we lose sight of our mission, and our team, so that we can avoid "giving up" on someone, we are failing as a leader.

Remember, all leaders are held to two standards: accomplish the mission and take care of our people. Meet these standards and we will be successful as leaders. Fail either one of them and we will fail as leaders. Mentoring, coaching, and commanding—and knowing when to do each—will help us do so.

Figure 38.3 Captain MacDonald aboard a V-22 Osprey, preparing for a mission overseas.

Note: Photo courtesy of Major Jake MacDonald, USMC.

Action Items on Developing Leaders

1. As the leader, stay focused on mission critical tasks. Delegate authority of as many other tasks to subordinates whose influence and leadership ability you wish to develop. Use the task/condition/standard process while doing so with them.
2. Get out from behind your desk, leave your office, and go talk to your team on a regular basis. If experiencing adversity as a team, do it even more. Leadership is a contact sport.
3. Figure out which members of your organization you've spent the most time mentoring. Have you seen a level of improvement in those individuals that would match the amount of time and effort you have invested?
4. Figure out which members of your organization have earned your time and mentorship. Are you giving it to them?
5. Are there members of your organization who provide value through their production but may not wholly fit your core values? It may be time to "invert the pyramid," and spend less time mentoring them and more time commanding them.

Saved Round on Developing Leaders

What is our biggest mistake? Despite our greatest efforts, we recruit and hire individuals who don't embody our team's culture. It is a mistake, but not our biggest mistake though.

Great leaders, mentors, and "life-changing" experiences can have a huge impact on individuals and teams. However, when we are asked, "Can you make someone more disciplined? More selfless? More [insert Core Value here]?" our answer is very simple: yes. Yes, we can and should make a positive impact on everyone with whom we associate and whom we lead. However, the values

(continued)

Saved Round on Developing Leaders (*Cont'd*)

we start with—the basic core values formed around the age of 10—are set by the age of 21.[2]

Rather than expecting to change everyone, have consistent Core Values and recruit individuals who already possess and exemplify them. We will end up expending a lot less time, energy, and emotional capital, first to build and then to sustain our championship culture when the people within the organization embody our Core Values.

However, every coach and every business leader on every battlefield has recruited an extremely talented individual to their team who doesn't share that team's Core Values, such as, in The Program's case, Selflessness, Toughness, and Discipline. With guidance and leadership, a world-class culture, a strong mentorship program, and incredibly challenging shared adversity experiences with teammates who do embody that team's core values, that individual will become less selfish, less physically and mentally soft, and less undisciplined. Unfortunately, even with these improvements, it doesn't necessarily make them selfless, tough, and disciplined. This is also not our biggest mistake, though.

As leaders, regardless of the team or the battlefield on which we compete, we can invest money and time into our organizations. But very few of us have an unlimited amount of money to invest into making our organizations world-class, and none of us have an unlimited amount of time to do so. Whatever the size of our budgets, time is our biggest limitation. Most people choose how they want to *spend* their time. In contrast, the most successful people choose how to *invest* it.

As the leaders of our organizations, every minute of our time spent mentoring and attempting to improve an individual's behavior on our team is one less minute we can invest elsewhere. Like all investors, we invest most of our time (and money) into those we believe will give us the greatest return on that investment.

---

[2] https://trevor.help/part-2-series-on-values/.

Time spent with one individual is time we don't have to spend with another. Is that investment of time with that particular individual maximizing the return for our team?

Most coaches and business leaders invest most of their time in improving the behaviors of their highest performers, the individuals who have the greatest talent for that chosen battlefield. We understand and agree with this philosophy. Basic mathematics does too: in any investment, if we make our top ten percent five percent better, we get a much greater return than if we make our bottom ten percent five percent better.

Unfortunately, often the incredible amount of time we invest into improving the behaviors of some of our most talented performers does not return any positive benefit to the team. Our rate of return on that investment is zero! Furthermore, as it relates to time, there has also been an opportunity cost for that investment. We could have invested our time elsewhere, specifically on other members of our team. They may not have been our best performers, but our rate of return would have been greater than zero.

Thousands of factors affect how we spend our time, and we certainly don't recommend hiring and firing people indiscriminately. It isn't in the best interest for the individual or our own team. We do, however, remind leaders that our first responsibility is not to the individual, but rather to the team. When we forget this, it is our biggest mistake as leaders.

We accomplish nothing in our life as individuals. Everything we do is done as a member of a team and teams are composed of teammates and team leaders. We have established both who teammates and team leaders are, how we can develop our efficacy as either, and the standards to which we are held in those roles. Next, we will discuss how we prepare ourselves daily to fill either role, specifically, by being physically and mentally tough, not making excuses (and not letting others make excuses for us), and finally, by working hard.

SECTION

IV

Be Tough

AT APPROXIMATELY 5:30 A.M. on May 23, 2010, The Program founder and CEO, Eric Kapitulik, stood on the summit of Mount Everest, the world's tallest mountain.

To reach the summit, Eric had spent more than seven weeks acclimatizing on the mountain. He had endured weeks of cold, harsh weather, and a lack of sleep and oxygen. He had pushed himself to his physical and mental limits, losing more than 35 pounds. While climbing at 20,000 feet, he had been caught in an avalanche that killed one climber and seriously injured another.

During his ascent while attempting the summit, Eric had endured four days of almost continuous climbing in below-zero temperatures, consumed less than a few thousand calories, and barely slept. Then, it got difficult....

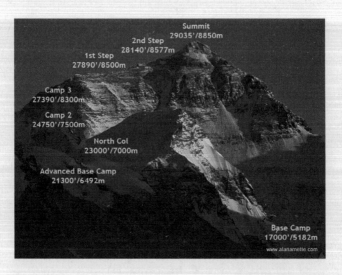

The route map up the northeast ridge of Mount Everest.

Note: Photo courtesy of ©Alan Arnette, www.alanarnette.com; reproduction prohibited without authorization.

39

Mount Everest: Facing the Challenge

AT 8,848 METERS (29,029 FEET), Mount Everest is the world's tallest mountain. Known as Chomolungma in Tibetan ("Mother Goddess of the Universe") it was first successfully climbed on May 29, 1953, by Sir Edmund Hillary, a New Zealand beekeeper, and Tenzig Norgay, a Nepali-Indian Sherpa mountaineer.

Prior to Mount Everest, Eric had spent a dozen years practicing the necessary skills required to safely attempt it. He had already summited four of the Seven Summits, the highest peaks on each of the seven continents. He had also climbed dozens of other major mountains throughout the world.

Eric's climbing career began while attending the U.S. Marine Corps' Summer Mountain Leaders Course (MLC) in Pickle Meadows, California. He had just returned from his first deployment overseas when his battalion sent him to this 8-week course where Marines who have attained a rank of sergeant or above are taught to become proficient in all the required skills to conduct mountain warfare operations. Eric attributes both his success as a climber and most importantly, his and his future mountaineering teammates' safety while doing so, to his weeks spent in Pickle Meadows.

These lessons taught by the Marine Corps, reinforced throughout his military career and then on mountains around the world, are one of the major differences between being a *good* teammate and team leader, and being a *great* one. These lessons separate great families, athletic teams, or corporations from simply good ones. They will allow us to achieve whatever our own personal summits may be. Our ability to learn and embody these lessons will be key in determining mission success or mission failure on whatever our chosen battlefield.

Specifically, mountaineering (and life) is challenging and dangerous. Our success in each is influenced by a host of circumstances that we don't control. Thankfully, we *do* control the greatest determining factor: our preparation. Not making excuses and working hard are big parts of our preparation (more on each in Sections 5 and 6), but our ability to do both is made possible only by our being physically and mentally tough. Our ultimate success in mountaineering (and life) is based not on our performance when *everything* goes well, but rather in those moments when little or *nothing* does; when we are faced with adversity. It is then then our physical and mental toughness will allow us to still attain the summits (and return to base camp safely) of the mountains in our own lives.

We will first briefly discuss the importance of physical fitness and the symbiotic relationship it shares with both physical and mental toughness. We will then define each and, most importantly, examine how we can all develop both within ourselves and our teammates.

40

The Case for Physical Fitness

WE ARE EXPECTED and required to behave and perform at a certain level at work, at home, in school, on our athletic teams, in civic organizations, and in the religious or spiritual community we associate with. To do so, to be great teammates and great team leaders on all the teams of which we are a part, requires an incredible amount of positive energy! Positive energy that we can give to our spouse, our children, and our coworkers. Positive energy that both our teammates and the mission deserve. Physical fitness provides it.

Mitochondria are energy-producing organs found in every cell of the body. As soon as we start to exercise, our body produces more of them. More mitochondria produce even more energy. This isn't something that The Program believes. This is what science teaches us.

For the purpose of this book, The Program considers a "fit" person to be strong, fast, and flexible, with good overall nutrition and wellness for their chosen sport, job, or lifestyle. It only makes sense that a very fit climber (with a lot of energy) will find climbing a mountain easier than a less fit one (who has less energy). It only makes sense that a fit athlete will find a workout or game less strenuous than an unfit athlete. The same is true regardless of the battlefield: a very fit Marine will not find a 20-mile hike or battle as difficult as an unfit Marine. A fit Fortune 500 salesperson or CEO will find a long, difficult business trip less strenuous than an unfit one. This is true for all of us, including being a fit husband, or wife, raising children.

147

Many of us will never find ourselves climbing one of the world's highest mountains, but we are all sons or daughters, husbands or wives, fathers or mothers. We are all members of a family, an athletic team, musical band, school, hospital, or corporate team. The fitter person will have more energy than the less fit one—energy we can invest in our own efforts at reaching the summits in our lives, and in our teammates who are attempting their own. All others things being equal, the more fit person will be a better teammate and better team leader than an unfit one.

So many things concern us. The most successful individuals and teams choose to stay focused only on that which they can control. We control our fitness level. Stay focused on it! The more fit we are, the more energy we have for all the battlefields we fight on, for the teammates we fight alongside, and the mission for which we fight.

The more fit we are, the more energy we have for all the battlefields we fight on, for the teammates we fight alongside, and the mission for which we fight.

Great fitness allows us to perform at or close to our physical and mental peak in perfect conditions. Unfortunately, Mt. Everest never has perfect conditions, and neither does life! Furthermore, regardless of how fit we may be, we will eventually face a type or level of adversity that we will not be able to overcome just because we have more energy. It is then that our physical and mental toughness will allow us to persevere, continue to make good mental decisions, and accomplish the mission.

Action Items on Physical Fitness

Growth or improvement in any aspect of our lives only occurs when we are outside of our comfort zone (i.e., outside of what we currently feel *comfortable* doing). Our physical fitness is no exception.

1. Know that you determine your fitness level and, regardless of its current level, you can improve it.
2. Set small goals. Most of us aren't *training* for something. We are *exercising* for life. We are all becoming more fit regardless

of the duration or intensity of the exercise. Set a goal to do it a few times for a little while every week. You can build from there.

3. Make a plan or enlist someone to help you do so. Stick to the plan. If you don't, shake it off and try again tomorrow. When *training for a race* or competition, a missed day can have dire consequences. When *exercising for life*, a missed day will have almost no consequence, unless it becomes two missed days in a row. And then three. And then . . . if you miss a day, reattack it tomorrow.

4. Tell family and friends about your fitness goals. Peer pressure helps. However, if our family and friends aren't helping us to become healthier human beings, we should spend less time with those family members and get different friends.

5. Do One More™! Review what you did during your last workout and then do it for 30 seconds longer or one rep more during this one. (There's more on One More™ in Section 6.)

6. Be committed. It is easier to be committed once we have made exercise a habit. Unfortunately, old, bad habits never completely go away, but thankfully we can create new, good ones. This takes more than a few weeks though. Commit to exercising for a month. Stay focused on doing it today. As entrepreneur and motivational speaker Jim Rohn said, "Commitment is doing what you said you would do long after the mood you said it in has left."

Saved Round on Physical Fitness

Ready!? Attack! Always remember that there is no true thing in life as "just maintaining." We are either getting better or we are getting worse. Compared to either our competition or, more importantly, the best version of ourselves, if we aren't becoming a better coach, doctor, lawyer, salesperson, parent, or spouse, we are becoming a comparatively worse one. The salesperson

(continued)

Saved Round on Physical Fitness *(Cont'd)*

who doesn't read how-to-be-better-at-sales books or who stops doing something to perfect their chosen craft is getting comparatively worse than the one who continues to improve. The same is true on any battlefield. As human beings, we hit our anabolic (strength) peak at approximately twenty-five years of age and our aerobic peak at approximately thirty-two years of age. "Just maintaining" our fitness after that and our bodies and fitness levels will naturally deteriorate. We get better or we become worse. There is no middle ground. Don't "just maintain" your fitness level and, most importantly, don't "just maintain" any other aspect of your life. Attack it!

41

Defining Toughness

EVERYONE IS A hero when it's seventy degrees and sunny. Unfortunately, that's not when you need them. We need great teammates and great team leaders when it's not! Plus, we have very few "seventy degrees and sunny" days; when everything goes exactly as we had planned. We don't control all the variables that would make a typical game or workday perfect. We never control the heat, the cold, the rain, the sun. We don't control an unexpected request from a client in Asia right before we are planning to leave for home or the amount of time our newborn baby slept through the night before our biggest presentation of the quarter. Games and workdays go into overtime. We have challenging personal and professional relationships and interactions. We face some form of adversity and a corresponding level of stress every day of our life. Physical and mental toughness allows us to remain the best teammates and best team leaders that we can be, regardless of these challenges.

Our physical fitness combines with our physical and mental toughness to make us as prepared as we can be to summit any mountain safely, battle our corporate opponents Monday through Friday, compete on Saturday or Sunday afternoon, and be the best spouses and parents possible. The best team leaders and the best teammates are tough—physically *and* mentally, not physically *or* mentally. (For the purpose of our book, The Program includes emotional resiliency as part of mental toughness.)

The Program defines "tough" as the ability to *withstand* and *attack* adversity or hardship while continuing to make good decisions that lead to

151

mission accomplishment. We also believe that being tough includes with-standing and attacking that adversity or hardship with a positive attitude (hence why we also include "emotional resiliency" as part of being a tough person). As the British Royal Marines' Commando Spirit highlights, being tough includes exhibiting a "cheerfulness in the face of adversity."

Based on personal experiences (like going to battle or climbing Mount Everest) and professional ones (annually working with more than 150 college and pro athletic teams and major corporations), our Program teammates know that "everyone is a hero when it is seventy degrees and sunny." Unfortunately, that's not when you need them. In fact, only when the conditions are *not* ideal do great teammates, great team leaders, and hence great teams prove just how great they are.

All of us, as individuals or as part of a team, will experience adversity during our season, fiscal year, or life: something or someone that challenges us, that causes stress and adversity. Our physical and mental toughness will determine if that adversity ultimately "beats" us or if we will still accomplish the mission.

Eric speaks to, and meets with, thousands of people annually. Most are familiar with the fact that he has summited Mount Everest. Inevitably, someone will remark to him that climbing Mount Everest is "all mental." Eric remarks with a laugh and a comment along the lines of "Yes, it is very challenging." What he thinks is, "Obviously, you have never climbed Mount Everest!"

Climbing Mount Everest is not "all mental"! All climbers are different, but Eric believes that climbing Mount Everest is 95% physical preparedness (fitness and physical toughness combined). The 5% mental is what will kill you, though.

Based on the teams of which we are privileged to be a part, the battlefields that we compete on, and the mountain summits we attempt to attain in our own lives, these percentages are different for all of us. For athletes, military members, and emergency first responders, mission accomplishment might require 50% physical preparedness and 50% mental toughness. Doctors, nurses, teachers, and business people might require a much greater percentage of mental toughness than physical for successful mission accomplishment. Regardless of the battlefield though, both physical and mental toughness will be required for us to be the best teammates and best team leaders that we can be.

Toughness is binary. It is a 1 or a zero. We are, or we are not, physically and mentally tough. Thankfully, both are learned traits.

42

A Light Switch, Not a Dial

PRIOR TO WORKING with our clients, The Program asks coaches and business leaders to fill out and return a Leadership Questionnaire (LQ). Our staff reviews these prior to the event in order to be as best prepared as possible. The LQ asks various questions about the team, including whether the team is physically and mentally tough. Often, coaches and business leaders will contact us prior to answering, explaining that they have team members who are tough, but when things "get bad," not so much. So the coach or business leader asks if they can put their team on a 0–10 scale. Our answer is always the same: no. Toughness isn't a dial; it's an on/off switch. It's binary, a one or a zero.

Someone who is a "one" (a tough person):

1. Has great habits
2. Makes good mental decisions regardless of the adversity
3. Is emotionally resilient; "cheerful in the face of adversity"
4. Craves a challenge

Someone who is a "zero" (not a tough person):

1. Has poor habits
2. Makes poor mental decisions when faced with adversity

3. Has no emotional resiliency: when things are good, they are happy
   and share their happiness. When things are bad, they are mad/sad/
   angry and they share their madness/sadness/anger.
4. Avoids adversity

We are or we are not tough. We can do tough things, show toughness, and exhibit the qualities of a tough person in a practice, game, or
business day. It doesn't make us a tough person; it just means that we
are doing something tough or being tough at that moment.

Toughness, like any Core Value, means we are tough all the time
and in everything we do. Selfless people aren't selfless only some of the
time or with certain people. If we are selfless with our own children but
not with the children down the street, we aren't a selfless person. We
just act selflessly with our own children. If integrity is a Core Value of
our team, then we act with integrity all the time. If we only act with
it some of the time, we aren't people of integrity. The same is true for
being kind, loyal, or any other Core Value. And toughness is a Core
Value. Not just when it is seventy degrees and sunny. Not just when
we feel like it. Not just when things are going well. Tough people are
tough all the time!

43

Toughness:
A Learned Trait

AFTER ALMOST EVERY single keynote address that he delivers, Eric is asked about climbing Mount Everest. Specifically, what is the toughest part of it? His answer is always the same: the first two days.

Mount Everest does not have perfect conditions. Even with global warming, it has never actually been seventy degrees and sunny. At high altitudes, our hearts must pump as much as twice as hard as they would at sea level for the same amount of oxygen. Caloric burn is based on many factors, but one of the main factors is heart rate. The faster the heart rate, the more calories burned. While climbing, an average climber will burn almost 10,000 calories per day on Mount Everest. At 6 feet tall and 210 pounds, Eric was burning almost 1,500 calories while sleeping at base camp—which has the best conditions on the entire mountain! You still have almost 15,000 feet of climbing ahead of you in atmospheric conditions that get exponentially more challenging, causing stress, pain, and discomfort. Climbers become frustrated and relationships with teammates can become strained.

Furthermore, most climbing enthusiasts have heard about the astronomical prices many people pay to summit Mount Everest. People may pay up to $200,000 to live in luxury accommodations at base camp, eating only the best food and having a team of Sherpas help them to the roof of the world. In contrast, Eric climbed Mount Everest for $17,000, including a $5,000 climbing permit. The remaining $12,000 was spread over two months on the mountain for food and base camp support. It did not include luxury accommodations. It included a small tent, where Eric slept inside a sleeping bag on a foam pad and 1-inch air mattress. His backpack was also his pillow. Meals, prepared by local Tibetans, were served in a communal tent with no heat, anchored into the ice of the Rongbuk Glacier. A sponge bath from a warmed pot of water was taken every 10–14 days. The toilet facility was a 5-gallon bucket.

Although they are Spartan accommodations, while en route from Kathmandu across the Tibetan plateau to base camp, climbers still have a bed and other basic, modern conveniences. Upon arrival at base camp, at a price of $17,000, none of those beds or other conveniences are available.

During the first two days at base camp, these conditions are at best annoying and at worst downright dangerous; when you wake up in the middle of the night at an altitude greater than 15,000 feet, it is minus 5 degrees and either you get fully dressed to go outside your tent to pee or risk frostbite on your private parts! In any event, by day 3, you don't even notice the lack of modern conveniences.

Tough times do in fact make tough people. The more experiences we have in putting our bodies in physically and mentally uncomfortable environments, the tougher we become. Our lives are fraught with tough moments already: having to fire an employee; playing without the star athlete; losing the job you've had for 15 years because of downsizing and having to find something new; struggling through IVF; or having a sick child or parent.

These tough, challenging events, or ones similar, will happen to us all. There is no reason to wait for them to occur before we become tougher. Do tough things now. Take the more challenging course in school. Ask to be responsible for the accounts whose clients are the most unreasonable. Take a public speaking course. Go for a walk in the rain. It doesn't need to be Mount Everest, and it doesn't matter how tough or not you are today. Just as we can train ourselves to be more physically fit, we can train ourselves to be more physically and mentally tough. Toughness is a learned trait.

Tough times, do in fact, make tough people. The more experiences we have in putting our bodies in physically and mentally uncomfortable environments, the tougher we become.

44

Developing Physical Toughness

ALTHOUGH FITNESS IS important, we are going to face some form and level of adversity that we will not be able to overcome just through our fitness, just because we have more energy. Our ability to still accomplish the mission will be dictated instead by our physical and mental toughness, and that of our teammates and team leaders. Therefore, regardless of the battlefields where we compete, the best teammates and best team leaders are both physically and mentally tough.

As previously discussed, based on Eric's experiences, personal strengths and weaknesses, and the realities of functioning in an extremely harsh environment like Mount Everest, he believes that climbing it was 95% physical and 5% mental. To accomplish the mission, he had to be extremely physically fit and physically tough. The 5% mental is what would have killed him, but the great proportion of his success on Mount Everest (and throughout his life) he attributes to the former. Based on our own experiences, strengths and weaknesses, battlefields that we compete on, and the summits we attempt to attain in our own lives, these percentages are different for each of us.

Athletes, members of the military, and the first-responder community might require an even split between physical and mental toughness. Others who typically work in climate-controlled offices might have a much greater need for mental toughness than physical for successful mission accomplishment. Although many of us may need our mental toughness to a much greater extent while pursuing mission accomplishment in an air-conditioned office, there will still be times in our lives when physical toughness is required.

Our office battlefields may not experience the same harsh weather conditions that are commonplace on Mount Everest, but we will all have long days and sleepless nights. We will still have mountains to climb and missions to accomplish when we are extremely tired. Physical toughness will help us to do so. Further, whatever the battlefield, we are all on a lot of teams. Regardless of the location of our work or the weather conditions it experiences, as a parent we will have an opportunity to go sledding with our children on an extremely cold day or play basketball with them on an extremely hot one. Our children or grandchildren will ask us to go outside and play. The more physically tough we are, the more we (and therefore, our child or grandchild) will enjoy the experience.

Following is how we ensure it.

Grind

The science of strength and conditioning is much more advanced than it was thirty-five years ago when Eric first started working out. Athletes are now told to "get on an end line" during conditioning. They are then instructed on how many sprints they are to accomplish, what the interval standard is, and what the rest period will be. Worse, we swim, bike, lift weights, walk or go for a run and we then determine its length and our pace by how we happen to be feeling during it. This does still produce better fitness, but it does not address our physical toughness at all.

Instead, put athletes on an end line during conditioning and tell them, "Run as fast as possible until we blow the whistle and then rest until we blow the whistle again. Repeat until we say you are done." That will make us fitter and tougher.

We don't need to be college athletes or have a certified strength and conditioning coach training us. We can do this for ourselves. At some point in any workout, when it gets challenging, demand more. Instead of doing 3 sets of 5 reps, do 2 sets of 5 reps and on the third and final set do as many reps as you possibly can. If we aren't lifting with a spotter who can help take the weight from our chest before the bar pins and crushes us to the bench, then we are not grinding.

Go to the gym with a workout plan in place. Then, add a 500-meter erg (row) as fast as possible between the heaviest sets of an exercise. Go for a walk with a distance and pace predetermined. When you get tired or arrive at the foot of a hill, make yourself run to the top of the hill. Think about what you don't want to do and then do it. What you don't want to do is what will make you tougher if you do it.

Grind.

The Upside of Deprivation

Water and food deprivation do not facilitate a great workout and we certainly do not condone, in any form, injuring or hurting any athlete (or yourself). However, while training, when you feel thirsty, try to do one more sprint or one more rep and then get that sip of water. This must be an individual effort. As a coach, if an athlete asks for water, there is only one answer: go and get it. If not, there are entirely too many bad things that can happen, and we don't truly know the extent of how hard everyone is pushing or what is going on internally with others. As an individual, however, we do! We know whether getting water now is a luxury or if it is a necessity. Can we safely push ourselves to do just one more sprint or finish the entire conditioning drill before we will need water? Train with the understanding that you can't tell the other team when to take a timeout just so you can get a sip of water.

We can deprive ourselves in other ways than just while working out. Pick a day and eat nothing for 24 hours. If you're a heavy coffee drinker, stop drinking coffee for a week. Deprivation makes us tougher.

Train How and Where You Will Compete

There is no bad weather. Just soft people.

Exercise in challenging physical environments. Train in the cold, in the heat, in the rain, and in the snow. Initially, you may very well not lift as much or run as fast as you could had you been inside. You will certainly not be as comfortable, but you will have made yourself physically (and mentally) tougher! We almost all live in places that can be extremely hot or cold. We will experience those extreme temperatures, even if only to walk to and return from our car, or watch our children play in an athletic contest. Train in the heat or cold and it won't feel as hot or cold when you are outside in it. Most people don't. Instead, if they exercise, they do so only inside a climate-controlled gym.

This isn't about becoming more fit. It is about becoming more physically tough. Remember, "there is no bad weather, just soft people."

For physical toughness workouts, visit www.TheProgram.org/athletics/ workouts.html.

Action Items on Developing Physical Toughness

We will all face some form and level of adversity that we will not be able to overcome just because we have the energy that physical fitness provides. More energy does not make bad weather more enjoyable. Further, there will be times when despite our best efforts, our energy will be depleted. We will be tired, but we must still accomplish the mission. Our physical toughness will allow us to do so.

1. Grind. Do whatever you do until it hurts and then keep going for just a little while longer.
2. Deprivation is a good thing. Deprivation makes us tougher. Deprive yourself of sleep, water, and/or food (ensure you are doing each sensibly once you know your body's ability to withstand each). When adversity strikes, we aren't necessarily given any of these, or certainly the amount that we would want. Prepare as if you understand and appreciate that.
3. There is no bad weather, just soft people. Exercise in—or at the very least, spend time in—an environment that is not climate-controlled. We all must work, play, and live with the weather during some part of almost every day. The more we train in it, the physically tougher we become.

Saved Round on Physical Toughness

Physically *fit* people train expecting the best. Physically *tough* people train while preparing for the worst. Fitness is incredibly important, and it will help us during a "perfect" game or business day. Unfortunately, we typically don't have many of those. A physically fit football player prepares for four 15-minute quarters. A tough one prepares knowing that a triple-overtime game could be the next one. A physically fit corporate teammate trains on days after eight hours of sleep and a good breakfast. A physically tough one trains every day, especially on the ones with no sleep while rushing to meet a deadline.

Always hope for the best. It facilitates a positive attitude. Always train while preparing for the worst. It facilitates mission accomplishment when it isn't seventy degrees and sunny. The greatest compliment you can receive when exercising is when someone asks you, "What are you training for?" and your only answer is "Life."

45

What Is Mental Toughness, and When Do We Need It?

THE COMPLEXITY AND power of our brains is barely understood. Many of us say that we are "freezing" when the temperature drops below sixty degrees. In temperatures and conditions that would cause most people to shiver uncontrollably, monks in the Himalaya steam wet towels dry. The process that enables them to do so is a particular form of meditation called g Tum-mo:

> The two aspects of g Tum-mo that lead to temperature increases are "Vase breath" and concentrative visualization. "Vase breath" is a specific breathing technique which causes thermogenesis, a process of heat production. The other technique, concentrative visualization, involves focusing on a mental image of flames along the spinal cord in order to prevent heat loss. Scientists at Harvard see the phenomenon as a profound example of the mind's ability to influence the body.[1]

Mental toughness is our ability to stay aware and focused in order to make good mental and emotional decisions, regardless of the stress and adversity facing us, and to do so with a positive attitude. Individuals can be very smart and get very good grades, but under pressure make poor decisions or become "frozen" with indecision. Mental toughness

---

[1] "Heat from Meditation," https://www.nytimes.com/1982/02/09/science/science-watch-heat-from-meditation.html, February 9, 1982.

162

allows us to make good mental decisions when we are experiencing either physical adversity (tired, cold, hot, hungry, thirsty, etc.) or mental adversity (mental fatigue; difficult interpersonal relations; lack of information, time, or a combination of both) and the resulting stress it induces.

Mental toughness is our ability to stay aware and focused in order to make good mental and emotional decisions, regardless of the stress and adversity facing us, and to do so with a positive attitude.

There are numerous occasions in which we make mental mistakes. The two most common occurrences are: (1) when we are physically tired, and (2) when we are under pressure or stress. These affect portions of every single day of our lives, regardless of our profession or the battlefields on which we compete.

We don't make mental mistakes in base camp. We make them on the descent from the summit. We typically don't make mental mistakes in the first quarter of a game. We make them in the fourth. We don't make mental mistakes at the start of our workday, after a full night of sleep and a large coffee on the morning commute. We make them after our kids were up sick all night. We make mental mistakes at the end of a long, difficult day. On whatever our chosen battlefield, we make mistakes when we are tired.

Unfortunately, we all work extremely long, challenging days—days that are stressful and physically, mentally, and emotionally draining. We are tired often. As discussed, any form of exercise creates a need for more energy—mitochondria are energy-producing organs found in every cell of the body. Exercise causes our body to produce more of them, and more mitochondria produce even more energy. More energy means that we feel tired less often. There is an important second benefit to exercise as well, which affects our mental toughness. When we exercise, we need to breathe more (and deeper) to provide our body with the increased oxygen that exercise requires. This causes an increase in our overall lung capacity. The greater our lung capacity, the greater the amounts of oxygen delivered to our brain and bloodstream during exercise, but also while at rest (e.g., while we are sitting at our desks working). The more oxygen in our brain and bloodstream, the more awake and alert we are.

The more awake and alert we are, the less often, and the shorter the duration, will our need be to tap into our reserves of mental or emotional toughness. The less we exercise, the less oxygen in our brain and bloodstream, and the less awake and alert we are. We will have to tap into our reserves for a longer period. If we want to make fewer mental and emotional mistakes, we need to be tired less often and have more oxygen in our brain and bloodstream. Exercise provides both.

Second, we make mental mistakes when we are under stress, when we feel pressure. This occurs numerous times every day in hundreds of different forms. We wake before the sun has risen to work out. We don't turn on any lights lest we wake up a sleeping child, or worse, a sleeping spouse. Walking across the living room, we step on a matchbox car that was left on the floor even though we have told our child a thousand times to put the toys away before going to sleep. Now we have to adjust our workout because any pressure on the right foot causes a pain to shoot into the lower back from the point of the heel where there is still an indentation from the matchbox car. We leave the gym to get a cup of coffee and there is a long line, and then we receive someone else's order. We are stuck in traffic on the way to an important morning meeting.

All this occurs before we have even arrived at work. Then come the inevitable difficult conversations with unreasonable clients or difficult co-workers—the same clients and co-workers who request additional work from us minutes before we are scheduled to leave for our son's wrestling match. The client wins. We are still at work. We arrive at home after the kids have gone to bed and the lights are off in the house. As we walk to the shower, we step on the same matchbox car.

Referees blow calls. Our starting quarterback, point guard, or pitcher gets injured. There are matchbox cars in all our lives. Mental toughness allows us to make good mental and emotional decisions when we encounter them. To ensure we do so, we must develop great habits, be passionate (not emotional), choose a positive attitude, and inoculate ourselves against stress. How to do so will be discussed next.

46

Don't Rise to the Occasion

SPORTS ANNOUNCERS LOVE talking about "rising to the occasion." They trot it out every week whenever an athlete has a big performance. However, for those of us in the military, law enforcement, or first responder communities, for those of us who have climbed Mount Everest, the idea that we will become more accurate with our weapon systems, quicker to diagnose injuries, more adept at reloading, better decision makers when we are exhausted in the Death Zone—in other words, that we will "rise to the occasion" just because we feel pressure—is ridiculous. This is not how our brains and bodies work. When adversity strikes, we don't "rise to the occasion." We sink to the level of our training. More specifically, we fall back on the habits that we have created right up until that moment.

> *In times of great adversity, we don't "rise to the occasion." We sink to the level of our training. More specifically, we fall back on the habits that we have created right up until that moment.*

The following is the Navy Cross citation for Sergeant Major Bradley Kasal:

> For extraordinary heroism while serving as First Sergeant, Weapons Company, 3d Battalion, 1st Marine Regiment, Regimental Combat Team 1, 1st Marine Division, I Marine Expeditionary Force, U.S.

Marine Corps Forces Central Command in support of Operation IRAQI FREEDOM on 13 November 2004. First Sergeant Kasal was assisting 1st Section, Combined Anti-Armor Platoon as they provided a traveling over watch for 3d Platoon when he heard a large volume of fire erupt to his immediate front, shortly followed by Marines rapidly exiting a structure. When First Sergeant Kasal learned that Marines were pinned down inside the house by an unknown number of enemy personnel, he joined a squad making entry to clear the structure and rescue the Marines inside. He made entry into the first room, immediately encountering and eliminating an enemy insurgent, as he spotted a wounded Marine in the next room. While moving toward the wounded Marine, First Sergeant Kasal and another Marine came under heavy rifle fire from an elevated enemy firing position and were both severely wounded in the legs, immobilizing them. When insurgents threw grenades in an attempt to eliminate the wounded Marines, he rolled on top of his fellow Marine and absorbed the shrapnel with his own body. When First Sergeant Kasal was offered medical attention and extraction, he refused until the other Marines were given medical attention. Although severely wounded himself, he shouted encouragement to his fellow Marines as they continued to clear the structure. By his bold leadership, wise judgment, and complete dedication to duty, First Sergeant Kasal reflected great credit upon himself and upheld the highest traditions of the Marine Corps and the United States Naval Service.[1]

Most people would say that Sergeant Major Kasal "rose to the occasion" that day. However, an iconic picture taken that day disproves this (see Figure 46.1). If you are ever watching an action movie and see the hero gripping a pistol, grinning menacingly with his finger wrapped around the trigger, that is a sure sign he knows nothing about firearms. Every member of the Armed Services has the four weapon safety rules drilled into him or her. First, treat every weapon as if it were loaded. Second, never point your weapon at anything you do not intend to shoot. Third, keep the weapon on safe until you are ready to fire, and four, keep your finger straight and off the trigger until you are ready to fire. These safety rules protect against a negligent discharge of a weapon (there is no such thing as an "accidental" discharge).

Look at the picture: Sergeant Major Kasal is near death, having just killed and having seen good men killed. His pants are soaked

---

[1] Navy Department Board of Decorations and Medals

Figure 46.1 Sergeant Major Bradley Kasal fell back to the level of his training during a surprise attack in Iraq.

Note: Photo courtesy of Lucian Read.

with blood from bullet wounds and from the fragmentation grenade he rolled on top of to protect his men. He still has his side arm out to provide cover for his Marines. Look closely at his pistol. Where is his finger? Straight and off the trigger. Even in the most stressful situation possible, he still did things "the right way." This isn't a fluke. He trained for thousands and thousands of hours to build effective habits. Sergeant Major Kasal didn't "rise to the occasion" that day; he sunk to the level of his training. However, the level of his training was so exceptionally high that he was still able to execute at an elite level in the face of extreme adversity.

This is why training is so important. The habits that we build in training are 100% the habits we will execute when "the bell rings." Many people cut corners in training. Athletes execute drills incorrectly or lazily, but they tell themselves, "It's only practice. I will do it right when it matters." They do not. Corporate teammates consistently send internal emails with spelling and grammatical errors, but tell teammates that they will correct the errors when the emails are sent to prospects or clients. No, they don't do that either. This isn't the way our brains work. There are no "gamers." Nobody will "rise to the occasion." Frankly, the idea that we can is an insult to the men and women who perform when it counts because they put in weeks, months, and years of sweat and tears to build great habits throughout their high level of training. They do so because they know at an instinctual level that in stressful environments, we don't "rise to the occasion." We fall back on our habits.

Mental toughness is a habit. Sergeant Major Kasal didn't have to choose to keep his finger off the trigger or risk shooting another Marine; he didn't have to make a good mental decision; it was simply a habit. If we have developed great habits, like keeping our finger straight and off the trigger until we are ready to fire, then when we are hit with the bullets and grenades we face in our own daily lives, we will still accomplish our mission.

47

Be Passionate, Not Emotional

MENTALLY TOUGH PEOPLE are emotionally resilient people. We all experience natural human emotions: happiness, sadness, anger, shame, and fear, to name a few. How we react to those emotions is a choice. Mentally weak people react in a manner that makes them feel better. Emotionally resilient, mentally tough people *choose* to react in a manner that will help their team accomplish its mission.

> *We all experience natural human emotions: happiness, sadness, anger, shame, and fear, to name a few. How we react to those emotions is a choice.*

Every coach in America tells us that their sport is an emotional one. Basketball is an emotional sport. Football even more so. You must play the game of soccer with great emotion. Business leaders discuss the "emotional meetings" they have. We hear it from coaches in every sport and business leaders in every industry, and we think, "Uh-oh."

Think about an emotional person whom you know, someone who reacts emotionally to life's various challenges. Think about someone with whom you recently had a disagreement, and remember how they reacted emotionally during your interaction with them. Close your eyes and picture that emotional person in that situation.

Now, ask yourself if you think positively or negatively about that person and if their emotional response helped the situation improve.

Uh-oh.

The Program loves passionate people.[1] We want to surround ourselves with people who are passionate about their spouses, children, jobs, and chosen pastimes. We appreciate the privilege we have of spending our time with young people who are passionate about football, soccer, music, art, or engineering. We are energized to work with corporate teams who are passionate about who they are and why they do what they do.

Close your eyes and think about someone who is a passionate person. What is your mental picture of that person?

Players, coaches, business leaders, or spouses aren't yelling and screaming *because* they are angry or upset. That would imply that you *had* to yell and scream when angry or upset. That's ridiculous. These are just emotional responses to the natural human emotion called anger. We all get angry. It is a natural human emotion just like happiness and sadness. However, how we respond to those emotions is a choice.

Football team A puts together a fourteen-play drive, scores a touchdown, and kicks off. Football team B takes it back for a 100-yard kickoff return touchdown. Team A's coaches are ripping their headsets off and throwing clipboards on the sideline. A spouse or parent is upset and starts yelling. There is no thought about what's in the best interest of the team and its ability to accomplish the mission—just emotion.

Mentally tough people are better than that—let our passion be driven by the mission and not by our natural, human emotions. In times of adversity, we want to surround ourselves with people who are mentally tough—people who are passionate but not emotional. What is the difference? One deep breath.

During that one deep breath, *think* (that is the keyword) about what your response should be to help your team accomplish its mission. There may still be times when a coach chooses to rip their headset off or throw a clipboard. Business leaders may still decide to gather their corporate team together and raise their voice over lack of effort, and a husband or wife may still decide to yell at their spouse or child,

---

[1] The Latin root of the word "passion" is *pati*, which means "to suffer." This meaning is mostly lost in common usage, but it still applies. To be truly passionate about something is to be willing to suffer for it. The suffering isn't meaningless. It is endured to further a cause.

but all are done after *thinking*: How do I respond to help my team get to a better place? How should I respond to my emotion in order to give my team the best chance of accomplishing the mission?

Leaders may still get it wrong. *Battle Leadership* is a collection of lessons learned by Captain Adolf Von Schell as a small unit infantry commander during World War I. In it he states, "Soldiers are not machines but human beings who must be led into war. Each one of them react differently, therefore each must be handled differently. Furthermore, each one reacts differently at different times and must be handled each time according to his own particular reaction."[2] So too do all of us. We work with and lead people, not machines. We all react differently at different times. As leaders and teammates, it is imperative that we have the ability to think prior to responding to ensure we interact with each of our teammates in a manner that best allows them, and our team, to accomplish the mission.

We are never guaranteed to make the right choice. However, choosing to *think* prior to responding certainly provides us with a better chance of doing so. The best teammates and the best team leaders are mentally tough, and mentally tough people are emotionally resilient. Emotionally resilient people, when faced with adversity, can think first.

Be mentally tough and emotionally resilient. *Take one deep breath.* Let our passion be mission driven, not emotionally driven.

---

[2] Captain Adolf Von Schell, *Battle Leadership*. Edited by Major Edwin F. Harding. (Fort Benning- Columbus, GA: The Benning Herald, 1933), 12.

48

Choose a Positive Attitude

BAD THINGS HAPPEN to us all. Mentally tough individuals have great, positive attitudes. They are cheerful in the face of adversity. This is a choice. As the saying goes, if you don't like where you are at, change your environment or change your attitude. Changing our environment can be very expensive and difficult. Changing our attitude costs us nothing and is easy to do. Choose to be positive! Positive is not happy. Happy is an emotion. Positive is a mindset.

One suggestion is to differentiate between what is "hard" and what is "challenging" in life. Eric has done one thing *hard* in his life. It isn't swimming out of a sinking helicopter while wearing 65 pounds of gear, weapons, equipment, and ammunition with no oxygen and no idea which way to swim to the surface, while drowning with a compound-fractured leg. Hard isn't racing in the Canadian Death Race Ultramarathon, finishing eight Ironman triathlons, or adventure-racing across various countries. It isn't undergoing the rigors of over a year of specialized military training before taking over his Force Reconnaissance Platoon of warriors, and it certainly isn't climbing Mount Everest.

On April 14, 2003, Corporal Jason David Mileo (USMC) was shot and killed while fighting insurgents in Baghdad, Iraq. Two days later and 6,000 miles away, Eric's commanding officer came to visit him in his office. He asked Eric if he would do him "a favor." His commanding officer couldn't order him to do what he was about to ask him to do. Eric had to agree to the role.

Fifteen minutes later, Eric left work, drove home, and changed into his Marine Corps Dress Blue uniform. He drove 60 miles to Centreville, Maryland, and proceeded up a long, winding gravel driveway. He parked his vehicle, walked to the front door, took a few deep breaths, and rang the doorbell. He stood there, waiting for the front door to open so that when it did, he could tell Corporal Jason Mileo's mother and father that their son had just died in Iraq.

The corporations, student-athletes, coaches, and teams with whom Eric has had the privilege of speaking are aware of Eric's accomplishments. As Eric is quick to point out, he has done one thing in his life that is *hard*. And it was *not* any of the things Eric has chosen to do. One time, he *had* to tell Leah Hall (Mileo) that her son had just died in Iraq. He had to ring the doorbell and wait, knowing that when the door opened, he was going to ruin Leah's life. He was going to deliver the worst news any parent could ever possibly receive. And he had no other choice. He had to ring that doorbell. He had to stand there and wait. As a Marine, he *owed* it to her son, whom he had never met, to tell his mother face-to-face what happened to him. He could not fake an injury and stay in the training room. He could not "call in sick." He had to do it.

If you have a sick friend, family member or teammate, or are dealing with the death of one, and you want to talk about how "hard" it is to do so, you will never get any argument out of The Program. We, however, take very strong exception to our clients talking about how "hard" it is to play at a particular "away" stadium, how "hard" it is to deal with a particular client, or how "hard" it was to wake up that morning and get to whatever playing field, battle field, or corporate board room you compete on or in.

Instead, change your mindset! What we do in our daily lives is not hard—it's *challenging*. Make it a habit to start thinking about those day-to-day things as such. Most of us perceive "hard" things as negative. Challenges are positive. We *have* to do things that are hard. We *get* to do things that are challenging. Happy, sad, and angry are emotions. We don't choose them. But positive is a mindset. We can choose it. Stop complaining. Focus on everything we do have in life and not what we don't. Our daily bumps in the road are not hard. They are challenging.

> *Happy, sad, and angry are emotions. We don't choose them. But positive is a mindset. We can choose it.*

Our thoughts become our words and our words become our actions. It's human nature that we just want to *get through* things that are hard, but as mentally tough warriors, we love to attack a challenge! Start to think about them as such. You will then talk about them as such, and you will then attack them as such.

Mentally tough people do not *get through*. They attack!

49

Inoculate Against Stress

We are all born physically and mentally soft. A baby zebra can get up and run on the Serengeti plains fifteen minutes after birth. It takes us more than a year to do the same. Most of us live in a country and grow up in families that afford us the luxury that when we are hot, we turn on an air conditioner, and when we are cold, we turn on a heater. That is not the case in most parts of the world. It just happens to be the case where we live, and for those fortunate enough to have the financial ability, where we vacation. We are born physically and mentally soft, and many of us remain soft throughout our lives. Then, so long as we have talent, we still do well. Many people do. However, to do *great*, to summit Mount Everest, or achieve whatever goals we set for ourselves, we must get comfortable being uncomfortable. We must inoculate against stress.

Mentally tough people understand that the more adversity they face, the greater their toughness. Just as every fall we get a flu shot—a small dose of the flu that helps our immune systems against the greater virus—we must do the same with stressful situations and adversity. We must find ways to inoculate ourselves against both. To do so, we must get comfortable being uncomfortable. We must get outside our comfort zone. If you find public speaking stressful, then take a public speaking course that forces you to speak in front of large groups. If making a cold call stresses you out, make a cold call. If a group fitness class frightens you or makes you uncomfortable, go take one. By doing so, we gain confidence, and because we gain confidence, we feel decreased levels of stress.

> *We must find ways to inoculate ourselves against stress. To do so, we must get comfortable being uncomfortable.*

Therefore, in moments that many people might feel are extremely stressful, mentally tough people, who have stress-inoculated themselves, simply won't feel the same level of stress as those who haven't. They don't have to be incredibly mentally tough in those situations that others find extremely adverse or stressful, because they find the same situation much less so.

As discussed earlier, after every Marine Corps (and most military) operations, units conduct a full debrief of the operation. At one, a pilot was telling another member of his squadron how everything was "screwed up" with the refueling of the aircraft and how the corresponding stress of it caused major issues for him. His teammate stopped him in midsentence and said, "That wasn't stressful! If you want to know stress, come to my house for dinner tonight and eat with my wife and eight kids. Then you will know stress!"

Dinner every night with his eight children had stress-inoculated that pilot so that his airplane not being refueled was just not that stressful. He was still able to stay aware of the environment and accomplish the mission. He was mentally tough. Admittedly, both pilots are probably mentally tough people. To do what they do requires it. However, when planes weren't being refueled, the pilot who stress-inoculated himself at dinner every night didn't require as much mental toughness as the pilot who hadn't.

This is true for all of us. We must stress-inoculate ourselves. If we don't have eight children all under the age of twelve, we must seek out adverse situations that force us outside of our comfort zone. Doing so increases our confidence and lessens the level of stress we feel when faced with adversity in the future. Like the pilot who's the father of eight children, we won't need to draw on great stores of mental toughness because we won't find the stressful situation that stressful.

50

Go or No Go?

Everest's north base camp is located at 17,400 feet. At altitudes greater than 14,000 feet, our bodies' ability to make proteins slows down and their break-down process increases. The result is that high-altitude climbers lose more muscle, faster.[1] Unlike a pre-race training period, when athletes are eating and training to ensure their best performance, as climbers gain elevation, their strength weakens. "If we lose ten pounds of weight at sea level, twenty percent of that would be muscle. If we lose ten pounds at 15,000 feet elevation, sixty-five percent of that would be muscle."[2] Mount Everest is 29,029 feet high.

Further, there is only 53% of the oxygen present at base camp as there is at sea level. At Mount Everest's summit, 36%.[3] However, although our muscular strength is decreasing the longer we stay at high altitudes, the opposite is true for our heart and lungs. By conducting acclimatization hikes and spending time at those higher altitudes, they become more efficient in using what oxygen is available. Eric was aware of this and, like most climbers, conducted four acclimatization hikes prior to his summit attempt.

---

[1] Peta Liston, "Preventing Muscle Loss During High-Altitude Exertion," https://healthcare.utah.edu/healthfeed/postings/2014/02/022614_high-altitude-muscle-loss.php, February 26, 2014.

[2] Ibid.

[3] "Altitude Air Pressure Calculator," http://www.altitude.org/air_pressure.php.

Fitness is still important, but when your battlefield causes 65% of any weight loss to be muscular and there is less than 40% of the normal oxygen available, physical and mental toughness will be required.

On May 18, 2010, Eric sat in Base Camp (BC) waiting to begin his summit attempt to the roof of the world. He had completed his fourth and final acclimatization hike more than a week prior. He had already been on the mountain for six weeks and hiked more than 110 miles all at an altitude greater than 15,000 feet during his acclimatization hikes just between Base Camp (17,300 feet) and Advanced Base Camp (ABC) located at 21,300 feet. He had ascended from Base Camp to the North Col, an elevation gain of almost 7,000 feet, more than three times and attained an elevation of 24,000 feet once. Climbers burn almost 10,000 calories per day while climbing at high altitude.[4] During his acclimatization hikes, Eric had lost more than 35 pounds. Regardless of how much you eat (and Eric's food selection was limited in what he and his teammates could afford), you simply can't eat enough to make up for the extreme number of calories your body is burning by just living at those high elevations, let alone while also conducting dangerous and strenuous acclimatization hikes.

Mount Everest's summit is located at the elevation in which the jet stream is normally located; winds during much of the year exceed 80 miles per hour, 6 miles faster than hurricane-force winds. The big question for climbers on Mount Everest (and throughout the entire Himalayas) is the timing of various weather patterns that bring reasonable winds for climbing (usually 25 mph or less) and in particular, summiting. It is never seventy degrees and sunny, but climbers want a three- to five-day period of *relatively* good weather at the extremely high altitudes of Everest during their summit attempt. Typically, this occurs during the second half of May. The problem is that this is not guaranteed. The jet stream can shift back and forth, and that three- to five-day weather window can close very quickly.[5]

Once it does and the monsoon hits, climbing ceases.

If and when to attempt the summit is always therefore a guessing game. An "educated guess" guessing game, but a guessing game nonetheless. Typically, climbers and guides are receiving weather

---

[4] Heer Khant, "10 Extreme Facts about Mount Everest," https://factsc.com/mount-everest-facts/, September 29, 2018.

[5] https://everestweather.com/.

reports for the high Himalayas from a few different weather forecasters. They do their best to piece those various weather reports together and then make an educated guess for when they should leave base camp, arrive on the summit, and return safely.

Eric and his climbing partner, Barry, waited in Base Camp poring over various weather reports in order to best-guess their own summit attempt during the normal, and expected, ten to fourteen days of good weather.

The monsoon was coming, though. The longer they waited for weather patterns that suggested good weather, the smaller their chances of getting to the summit prior to the full fury of the monsoon.

Making things more challenging for the weather forecasters, guides, and climbers throughout the Himalayas that year was that on April 14, Eyjafjallajökull, a volcano in southern Iceland, erupted. A 30,000-foot-high ash plume shot into the air. After 24 hours, the plume had risen another 6,000 feet and eventually covered an area nearly the size of Western Europe.[6]

At the time, it was determined that the eruption of Eyjafjallajökull had changed the weather patterns on Mount Everest. Instead of approximately two weeks of good climbing weather, with a three- to five-day window of light winds on its summit, the expedition determined that the mountain would probably experience two smaller windows of good weather overall and only a day or two of light winds on its summit.

Regardless of the mountains we are attempting to climb in our own daily lives, we never have all the information, and often we don't even have as much of it as we would like. This is true if we are trying to decide when to depart base camp to summit Mount Everest, or when to deploy capital for a project or business venture. It is true when we are in a game and our opponents do something that had not been covered in a scouting report or at practice. It is certainly true for the many decisions parents are faced while raising their children.

We all experience moments in our lives when we don't know what we should do with absolute certainty. Mentally tough people do not wait for absolute certainty before making a decision. They know that that level of certainty will never occur. Instead, mentally tough people make an educated guess, an educated decision, and then they do everything humanly possible to make that decision the right one.

---

[6] Iceland on the Web, https://www.icelandontheweb.com/articles-on-iceland/nature/volcanoes/eyjafjallajokull/.

51

Go!

ERIC AND BARRY had to decide if they would be able to attempt the summit and return safely in a severely truncated amount of time, knowing that any mistake could prove fatal. They decided to try. Eric had learned twelve years earlier at the military training center at Pickle Meadows that mountains kill people, just not as often as climbers' own bad decisions do. As physically and emotionally drained as they were going to be, he knew that they would have to be physically and mentally tough.

On May 19, 2010, Eric and Barry left Base Camp. Instead of a summit attempt and safe return in 10 days, they planned on 5–6. To do so, they would have to draw on every ounce of physical fitness and physical and mental toughness that they possessed. They left BC and hiked to Advanced Base Camp (ABC), covering the 12 miles and 4,300 feet of elevation gain in just over 5 hours (the average is 8 to 10 hours). Typically, climbers spend a day or two at ABC prior to continuing up to Camp 1 at 21,000 feet. Eric and Barry spent 6 hours. They reached Camp 1 after 3 hours of climbing (the average is 4–6 hours), ate one packet of oatmeal each, slept, and pushed on. They reached Camp 2 at 24,750 feet in 3.5 hours (the average is 5–6 hours). They split a protein bar, slept briefly, and continued forward and up. Always up. They reached Camp 3 at 27,390 feet, high into the Death Zone, 3 hours later (the average is 4–6 hours).

They arrived at Camp 3 at 3:32 p.m. on the afternoon of May 22. Most climbers will begin their summit attempt from Camp 3 at 1:00

or 2:00 a.m. in hopes of reaching the summit early in the morning to enjoy the views. Most importantly, it also provides them with as many daylight hours as possible, should something go wrong in descending the mountain. If you are caught outside your tent at night in the Death Zone, with dwindling oxygen, your chance of frostbite is 100% and survival is almost zero.

Eric and Barry discussed how they were feeling physically and mentally. Both felt okay, or at the very least, as well as someone could feel after 4 days, almost no sleep, two packets of oatmeal, two protein bars, and a few pieces of mini dark chocolates. They were both concerned about the possibility of worsening weather on the mountain and being held up by slower climbers on the upcoming three "steps," sections of almost vertical climbing that must be overcome a few hours after leaving Camp 3.

They made their decision—a mentally tough decision that would require them to prove their physical toughness. They wanted to stay and rest. Instead, they chose to leave as soon as possible. Based on their previous movements on the mountain, in doing so, they would summit in the middle of the night. Although saddened that they would not see the views from the summit, the risks of worsening weather and other slower climbers impeding their movement on the mountain was too great. They would reach the summit, take what photos they could, vouch for each having made it, and descend as quickly as possible. They stayed focused on mission accomplishment. Mentally tough people do so regardless of the adversity.

Regardless of how physically fit we may be, at some point we all get tired. When we do so, we then must remain alert and responsive to a changing environment and the challenges inherent in it. In our daily lives, we all want to sleep. We all get frustrated and worn down. We all get sad, happy, or mad depending on the circumstances, and we all want to cry, laugh, or scream out loud. Can we put all of that aside and remain focused on doing what is in the best interest of the team for it to accomplish the mission?

Mentally tough people stay focused on the mission regardless of the adversity.

52

The Death Zone

ALL MOVEMENTS, INCLUDING boiling water, are incredibly difficult in the Death Zone—altitudes greater than 26,000 feet. The Death Zone is aptly named; if climbers stay too long at those extreme altitudes, they die.

Eric and Barry wanted to lie down and rest, but instead forced themselves to cook and share one more packet of oatmeal, knowing that any calories consumed now would be used as fuel later in the day by their bodies. No oatmeal now would mean their bodies consuming even more of their muscles in the oxygen-depleted landscape. As explained earlier, an average climber will burn 10,000 calories per day climbing on Mount Everest. In the Death Zone, that number sky rockets to 20,000 calories.[1] After eating and filling up their water bottles with the remaining water, without sleeping or rest, they departed Camp 3 for the summit at 6:35 p.m. that evening.

The "best shape of your life" is not good enough for Mount Everest if that "shape" is not good enough to handle the physical challenges that climbing the world's tallest mountain will demand. Instead of the best shape of your life, arrive at base camp in "Everest Shape," as Mount Everest expert Alan Arnette says. Eric ensured it. He was 37 years old. For years leading up to his Everest expedition, he consistently worked out six days every week: lifting, swimming, biking, and running. A

---

[1] Heer Khant, "10 Extreme Facts about Mount Everest," https://factsc.com/mount-everest-facts/, September 29, 2018.

typical week would consist of at least two weight lifting workouts, 5–6 miles of swimming, 20–30 miles of running, and 60–80 miles of biking. Eric had always been in great physical shape. He ensured that for this expedition, he would be in "Everest Shape."

In the first six weeks since arriving at Mount Everest base camp, even this mountain had been his playground. As soon as he departed Camp 3 for the summit, he knew that it no longer would be.

After less than 100 meters, Barry had to stop and wait for him and asked if he was feeling all right. Eric told Barry that he felt okay, but just could not move at the same pace he had been climbing in all his previous climbs. Experienced climbers will tell you that during any expedition, they have good days and some not so good ones. Eric immediately knew that today, the most difficult day of the expedition, was going to be his first "not so good one" in seven weeks. He also knew that he couldn't remain in the Death Zone: either he would have to attempt the summit or return immediately to lower elevations. Eric knew it was going to be a very long night. He was already tired. After weeks of cold, harsh weather, lack of sleep and proper nutrition, all while exerting himself mightily in the acclimatization hikes and this summit attempt, he would have to be physically and mentally tough.

Eric gained the summit ridge ten hours after leaving Camp 3, three hours more than he had expected. At 4:35 a.m., it was still dark. It was minus 50 degrees. Years of training in Marine Corps Special Operations and pushing himself to his limits, both physically and mentally, had provided him with a thorough understanding of the capabilities of his body and his mind. He was physically and mentally tough. He would need both. Every step had to be evaluated and placed appropriately. Eric continued to the summit agonizingly slow, ensuring that every foot placed in the snow, ice, and rocky ridge was secure to avoid a fall thousands of feet down the Kangshung Face, a 2,000-foot sheer drop. Climbers must hike its knife edge to gain the summit.

We may never find ourselves actually in the Death Zone, a place where if we stay too long, very bad things will happen to us, even death. We may never actually be above 26,000 feet on the side of a Himalayan peak, but there will be times in our life when we will feel that we are: our company files for bankruptcy, we are fired from a job, we are taken advantage of by a person we trusted, lies are told about us, we are made fun of or called "weird" by people who aren't cool, by any standard, but we are too young to understand that, or we experience the ultimate tragedy, the death of a dear friend or family member. In those moments, if we have made ourselves as physically and mentally tough as possible and have surrounded ourselves with people who have done the same, we can and will keep climbing!

53

The Summit, but Not Mission Accomplishment

ERIC GAINED THE summit at 5:26 a.m. Three minutes later he watched the sunrise over Nepal and Tibet. He thought of Major Douglas Zembiec (USMC),[1] a fellow Naval Academy classmate, an All-American wrestler, and his best friend. They had talked often of climbing Mount Everest together. Doug had been shot and killed in Iraq while conducting clandestine operations three years earlier. Eric sat on the summit and thought about him. He wept.

Although he had reached its summit, Eric knew that he had not accomplished the mission and could not remain. The mission was to gain the summit *and* return safely. After six minutes, Eric took one final view from the summit and started back down the mountain, racing against the bad weather expected later that day.

Walking back to Camp 3, Eric had not slept in almost 36 hours and had slept only briefly in the previous five days total. He had eaten less

---

[1] The Doug Zembiec Award is presented annually for outstanding leadership in the Special Operations Community. Interestingly, it was Major General Paul Lefebvre, then the Commander of Marine Corps Special Operations, who chose the award to be named after Doug. Earlier in his career, Lieutenant Colonel Lefebvre was Ray Lipsky's Battalion Commander who spoke of a man being a sum of his experiences (Chapter 3).

than one thousand calories during that time, while his body consumed ten, fifteen, and twenty times that amount each day. He was exhausted. With the Kangshung Face on his immediate right and his crampons (ice screws attached to the bottom of climbing boots) slipping on the rocky knife-edge ridgeline, he would continuously start to think about food, in particular, the fish tacos that he wanted. Technical sections required him to clip and unclip carabiners to fixed ropes, ensuring that should he fall, at the very least, he would fall only a few hundred feet rather thousands. He was exhausted, but he had to continue to make good mental decisions. He wanted to unclip all his carabiners and just walk down the mountain. Instead, he fell back on his habits while also continuously reminding himself to slow down and remember the mission, not the fish tacos. Mountains are dangerous and can kill you, just not as often as climbers' own bad decisions do.

Eric gave himself small goals. The goal was not to get back to the safety of Camp 1 8,000 feet below. That was too overwhelming. The goal was to get to "that rock!" That rock might have been 50 feet away. As he continued down the ridge, the new "rocks" became 40 feet, and then 30 feet, 20 feet, and finally, Eric was giving himself goals of reaching points on the mountain 10 feet away in an effort to keep himself "dialed in" and making good decisions. After 3 hours (the average is 7–8), Eric reached Camp 3, and he and Barry immediately continued their descent.

They reached Camp 2 at 2:00 p.m. Although at a relatively low altitude of 24,750 feet, Camp 2 is horribly exposed to high winds. With wind speeds in excess of 40 miles per hour and increasing, Eric and Barry stopped to collect the gear that they had left there on the way up the mountain 24 hours prior and continued to Camp 1, 1,500 feet below. Nighttime was falling. It was bitterly cold and windy as they stumbled down the long, exposed, snowy slope. To sit down and fall asleep in the snow was death. They were exhausted, and if they both fell asleep, they would never wake up; they would die from exposure to the unrelenting wind and cold buffeting them. Instead, they took turns doing so. One climber would sit, while the other stood. They would allow rest stops of no more than three minutes. When it was one climber's turn to sit, they fell asleep almost before they had completely sat down. After 180 seconds, the standing teammate would force the sitting climber to wake and then both would continue down the slope until the next stop, when they switched responsibilities.

On Mount Everest, at school or at work, and while at play, be sure to associate and team with other great teammates who are physically and mentally tough. We will face adversity throughout our lives and when we do so, tough teammates really help.

54

Mission Accomplished

ERIC AND BARRY reached Camp 1 at 21,000 feet at 9:00 p.m. They had been climbing almost continuously for two days. Pausing only long enough to remove their crampons, they climbed into their tent, laid a sleeping bag over themselves as they huddled together, and immediately fell fast asleep. Eric awoke two hours later with snow falling on their tent. Eric still does not recall what caused him to wake as the snow was not loud and he was already at his emotional, physical, and mental limit. He woke Barry and asked him what he thought they should do: continue to sleep, wait until morning, and then descend from Camp 1, or "suck it up" and depart as quickly as possible. Both were concerned about the new snow falling on the steep climb up to Camp 1 from Advanced Base Camp. One month earlier, Eric had been caught in an avalanche that killed another climber in that exact location. Although physically and mentally exhausted, they decided to dress (put their crampons on), pack the remaining gear that they had cached on their way to the summit, and descend. It was a mentally tough decision that required great physical toughness.

Eric recalls that shortly after they had started their descent, the snowstorm abated, and a full moon came out from behind the clouds. The full moon was so bright and, with no ambient light so deep in the vast Tibetan mountain wilderness that they shut off their head lamps and descended all the way back to the foot of the mountain with only the moonlight showing their way. Even exhausted, Eric remembers the descent down the face of the mountain bathed in the yellow glow of a full moon over the Himalayan peak. It is an image he will never forget.

They reached the foot of the mountain and Advanced Base Camp (ABC) shortly thereafter. It was now 6:00 a.m. Their support crew of Tibetan cooks welcomed them back from the summit with singing, dancing, and the banging of pots. Hugs and handshakes were given all around. Their plan was to spend the day and a night at ABC before returning to Base Camp, 12 miles and 4,000 feet of elevation below. They sat down to eat their first real meal in six days. Eric remembers stuffing food into his mouth. He was ravenously hungry. The kitchen tent was warm from the propane stoves used to boil water and cook the food. Immediately, Eric ran from the tent and was sick in the snow. He returned to the tent feeling bad lest he unwittingly insult the Tibetan cooks who had labored over this "successful summit" meal. He again tried to eat and again needed to run out of the tent. Barry was feeling the same.

Now they had to determine what to do next. Exhausted from almost fifty straight hours of climbing, Eric and Barry decided to continue their descent to base camp right away, hoping that the additional drop in elevation would allow both to feel better. Once more, they repacked their backpacks and began the 12-mile trek down to base camp.

Almost two miles up the Rongbuk Glacier from base camp, Eric and Barry could see the lights on inside of the tents of climbers who had decided to wait for a longer weather window (which ultimately, they did get). Nighttime had descended upon them as they hiked down the glacier. Eric, at this point, was stumbling down the mountain, wanting only to get to as low an elevation as possible, as quickly as possible, and give his body an opportunity to recover.

As he came around a turn in the trail, he was met by one of the Austrian climbers whom he had befriended during the seven weeks on the mountain. The Austrian had been listening to the radio traffic between base camp and the two climbers and knew they were descending. Eric saw him sitting on a rock along the trail with his head lamp on. At first, as Eric recalls, he thought that it was a climber heading to Advanced Base Camp, but then just as quickly dismissed the idea, as no climber would be starting their hike to ABC that late at night.

Figure 54.1 Author and Program founder Eric Kapitulik, upon returning to base camp from the summit of Mt. Everest.

As Eric came upon him, the Austrian climber congratulated Eric with a handshake and a hug. He then said to Eric, "I thought you might be needing this," and handed him an ice-cold Coca-Cola.

As soon as the soda entered his mouth, with its combination of sugar and caffeine, the world immediately got brighter, birds started chirping, and music started playing. Eric looked at the Austrian climber and told him, "Axel,[1] I am going to name my first son after you." Eric, Axel, and Barry walked the final two miles to base camp together. They had done it (Figure 54.1).

Sixteen months later, Axel Douglas Kapitulik was born.

Action Items on Mental Toughness

Mental toughness is an ability to stay aware and focused in stressful environments. It includes an ability to make good mental and emotional decisions regardless of the stress and adversity facing us and to do so with a positive attitude.

---

[1] Axel Naglich is a former Red Bull Extreme Skier from Kitzbuhl, Austria.

1. Exercise. It gives us energy, which helps with fatigue and causes our heart and lungs to pump more oxygen to our brain which helps us stay mentally "dialed in."

2. Create good habits. In times of great stress, we do not "rise to the occasion." We "fall back" on the habits we have created right up until that point. Develop better habits so that when we are under stress, we don't have to *make* good mental or emotional decisions—we do them habitually.

3. Be passionate, not emotional: We all have emotions. That is normal and we don't control them. Mentally tough people choose how they respond to them, though. For example, we don't yell because we are angry. We are angry and we yell. When mentally tough people experience a certain human emotion, they take one deep breath and think about how they should respond to that emotion in order to help their team accomplish its mission.

4. Mentally tough people have a positive attitude. We control very few things in life, but our attitude is one of them. Are we choosing to be an energy giver or an energy vampire? Energy givers are great teammates and team leaders. Vampires are not. As a suggestion, the next time someone asks you how your day is going, put a smile on your face and respond, "I have never had a better day in my life!" If it doesn't put a smile on their face, that person is an energy vampire. Regardless, you will have a more positive mindset because of doing so.

5. Our thoughts become our words and our words manifest themselves in our actions. Think positive thoughts. Your words will be positive and then so will your actions. It works in the opposite direction too. If you are having a bad day—as we all do from time to time—act in a positive manner. This can manifest itself in many ways, but for a start, smile. You will talk positively and then you will think it too.

6. Mentally tough people inoculate themselves against stress. They still feel stress, just not as much as others who have not inoculated themselves against it. Do things that are a little stressful. They allow us to deal with and attack the big stressful things better.

Saved Round on Mental Toughness: A Note from Program Founder Eric Kapitulik

I am constantly questioned about why I would climb Mount Everest, or any mountain, for seven weeks to spend only six minutes on its summit. I love nature and being outside. I love the opportunity that climbing provides me to travel to places that I could only read about as a child. I find it incredibly interesting to meet and get to know people from countries other than my own and the perspective it provides me. I enjoy all these things, but that is not why I climb. I could enjoy all these things while not destroying myself physically on the side of a wind-swept, icy mountain slope in freezing temperatures.

I climb to test myself. I enjoy doing so. Climbing Mount Everest (or any really big mountain) tests my physical and mental toughness. I believe that both have been vitally important to my success and the teams of which I am privileged to be a part. While climbing, I get to prove that toughness—to myself. I don't always love the misery inherent in climbing. I do love that it affords me an environment where I am able to prove that I am physically and mentally tough—at least for those seven weeks while climbing.

I appreciate that many people will still never understand why anyone would ever climb a mountain for seven weeks for *only* six minutes on the summit. I understand and appreciate why people wouldn't do it. I am just grateful I am not one of them. I had six minutes!

There are a handful of select climbers who have climbed Mount Everest without the aid of supplemental oxygen, a guide, or Sherpas. For the rest of us, we have all used them in our attempts on the world's highest peak. Does it diminish the accomplishment? That is for the reader to determine. I have not mentioned my climbing Sherpa partner, Kaji, or any other members of the expedition except for Barry, whom I was constantly with on the mountain during our acclimatization period and the entirety of our summit attempt. I could not have done it without Kaji, but he was not with me throughout the entire expedition and I felt it would be confusing to the reader to continue to mention when he was present and when he was not. I am eternally grateful for those six minutes on the summit and to all the people who made it possible, though Kaji, especially.

As I have matured, I appreciate that being the best husband to my wife and father to my children allows me to test my toughness, as well. As NFL Hall of Fame running back Barry Sanders once said, "I spent most of my life trying to be *the* man. Now, I am just trying to be *a* man."

What mountain is next? Whatever mountain my son, daughter, or wife want to climb with me. Climbing big mountains is terribly time-consuming. It is definitely not "out of my system," though. I still love doing it—just not more than spending time with my family. The next big mountain I climb will be with one or all of them.

SECTION

V

No Excuses

AN IMPROVISED EXPLOSIVE device (IED) can be detonated in a variety of ways. This IED was "command detonated." A wire connected it to a device held by an insurgent hiding down the street in a building. He waited and watched as Sam got closer and closer to it: three 105 mm anti-aircraft rounds bound together and buried in the road. Each round was 3 feet long and weighed over 30 pounds. It was packed with nails, screws, and other deadly bits of metal and glass to serve as shrapnel. As Sam approached, the insurgent pressed the button on the device, and Sam's life changed forever.

Sam Cila not making excuses as he grabs, lifts, and flips a 400-pound tire—with one hand.

Note: Photo courtesy of Eric Kapitulik.

195

55

No Excuses

WHEN THE IED detonated, the blast blew Sam Cila's 230-pound body 15 feet into the air and 25 feet down the road. Shrapnel raked the left side of his body and ricocheted off his ceramic chest plate, shearing off most of his left bicep and triceps. Sam's brachial artery was severed a half inch from his heart. As Sam lay in the street dying, an AK-47 round ripped through his left leg.

Sam Cila sat up and fought back: firing one single round from his M-4 carbine before collapsing back into the dirt.

Great teammates and great team leaders do not make excuses. Unfortunately, not everyone is a great teammate or great team leader. Here are some excuses that we hear all the time:

I don't work out: I don't have enough money to join a gym. I don't have the time. I'm married. My wife doesn't work out. I have kids. I work a lot. I'm too old.

I can't lose weight: My wife cooks unhealthy meals. I'm too busy. I am always traveling for work.

I didn't get the report in on time: I was so busy. My kids were sick. My alarm didn't go off. I had an emergency.

We didn't reach our sales goal: It's a bad economic environment. The prospect isn't very smart. He doesn't call me back. She doesn't

197

answer my emails. Our technology isn't as good as our competitors'. We don't have enough people. Our marketing is poor.

We lost: It was a bad call by the referee. Jimmy was injured. Jane wasn't there. It was too hot. It was too cold. It was exam week.

These are all excuses. An excuse is nothing more than an admission that we failed to prepare properly. Every single excuse listed could have been overcome with proper preparation.

An excuse is nothing more than an admission that we failed to prepare properly.

56

A Life-Changing Explosion

I<small>N 2007, SAM</small> C<small>ILA</small> deployed to Iraq with the "Fighting 69th," a National Guard unit from New York. Sam's platoon was hand-selected to work under and support 5th Special Forces Group. As part of this support, they executed a raid in the town of Amaria and managed to capture a few high-value insurgent leaders. The next day, Sam's platoon was tasked with going back to the town to talk to the villagers and see if they could glean any more intelligence. They rolled in on armored vehicles, but dismounted outside the village and moved in on foot. Armored vehicles offer greater survivability, but you are far less likely to see or hear possible threats. In addition, the threatening look of the powerful vehicles often intimidated the locals, who were therefore more reluctant to speak to them. Sam and his teammates moved into the town with the vehicles rolling slowly behind them.

Looking for threats, and possible improvised explosive devices (IEDs), is physically and mentally exhausting. You are constantly searching for items that seem out of place or were not there earlier. Unfortunately, roadsides are strewn with piles of garbage and refuse, and it is tough not to "see an IED" everywhere you look.

While scanning the area, Sam noticed a pile of garbage that had not been there the day prior. Sam and his teammates approached the suspicious area to investigate further. When the insurgent detonated the IED, the blast was enormous. It blew a hole in the concrete street 3½ feet deep and 12 feet across. Sam was approximately 75 feet away when the device exploded. Shrapnel flew across Sam's body from the right side and ricocheted off his ceramic chest plate, shearing off most of his left bicep and tricep and severing his brachial artery a half inch from his heart. He also took severe shrapnel damage all along the left side of his body. As soon as the IED exploded, the attackers also opened up with machine gun and small arms fire and Sam took an AK-47 round through his left leg.

After being thrown to the ground, Sam was able to sit up and fire one single round from his M-4 rifle before collapsing to the dirt. He watched in surreal horror as his now severed brachial artery spurted blood over his head in high arching streams. Reacting quickly, his teammates were able to fight through the ambush and provide Sam with lifesaving care. He was evacuated back to his base and from there to Landstuhl, Germany, for further care. However, Sam's fight was far from over. In Germany, a nurse mistakenly double tapped his morphine drip. The resulting flood of narcotics caused Sam to overdose and put him into respiratory arrest. He was given Narcan (a drug used to reverse/combat opioid overdose) and a breathing tube. This extended his stay in Germany for two days before he was flown back to the states for further treatment.

Back at Walter Reed National Military Medical Center—known as Walter Reed Hospital—in Bethesda, Maryland, Sam underwent over 40 surgeries to correct the damage he sustained in the explosion, including having a plastic stent put in near his heart so that blood could still flow to the left side of his body. He needed multiple surgeries just to remove all the dirt, metal, and debris embedded in his body.

Even after multiple surgeries, Sam was left with, what he called, a "lifeless claw." Because of the severe nerve damage in Sam's arm, it proved almost impossible to regain functionality in his hand. Doctors tried everything. Eleven surgeries on his hand and forearm proved unsuccessful. They moved muscles around, separated and reattached tendons, and even used metal and springs in an attempt to provide Sam with a working hand. All to no avail. He pulled the muscles, snapped the tendons, and broke the springs. It seemed that each successive surgery mangled his hand even more. In addition, because of the nerve damage and restricted blood flow, simple injuries like cuts, scrapes, and burns took incredibly longer to heal than they should have.

During the fifteen months that Sam spent at Walter Reed, he had the opportunity to meet countless veterans who had lost a limb completely and seemed to be adjusting more quickly to the adversity than he was. The final straw came when Sam and his family went to a Korean barbecue restaurant that had a small grill embedded in the table for diners to grill the meat to their liking. Before dinner, without knowing it, Sam placed his hand on top of the hot grill. He never felt the grill as it seared his flesh. It wasn't until Sam noticed the scent of burning flesh, an aroma that most combat veterans are unfortunately familiar with, that Sam pulled his hand off the grill, though not before sustaining third-degree burns. In that moment, Sam decided to have his left hand amputated.

The recovery process was brutal. Sam experienced excruciating pain and crushing setbacks. He needed to relearn how to do everything from getting dressed and shaving to driving with one hand. To complicate matters, his doctors' primary method for helping him cope with the pain from recovery was to prescribe Sam a bevy of painkillers. As many veterans and other trauma survivors can attest, although the painkillers can do a great job of deadening the physical pain, they can also deaden your other feelings; feelings like love, motivation, and resolve. Further, they only increase your desire for more painkillers. Over time, doctors prescribed more and more painkillers to help Sam cope with the pain of his injuries. As his setbacks piled up and simple activities became more difficult, Sam did what many people do. He made excuses.

Working out was too hard now. How was he supposed to dead lift or ride a bike with one hand? The medications he took sapped his energy. How could he be expected to play with his sons or be a good husband when he could barely get off the couch? Most of us will never experience that kind or level of adversity. However, those excuses snowballed and dragged him even further into a dark place.

To make matters worse, the people around him made excuses for him as well. Their excuses all came from a place of love. After what he had been through, and what he was currently going through, it was impossible for his loved ones to tell him to "snap out of it" and stop feeling sorry for himself.

Sam's mindset finally began to change when some of his teammates from the military visited him. They took one look at him lying on the couch, an unmotivated, out-of-shape shell of what he once was, and told him what he needed to hear. They told him to get off the couch and get back in shape. They told him to stop making excuses for himself. Sam thought about their words, about the adversity he had faced, and the long road ahead of him. Most importantly, he thought about the example he was setting for his two sons. He decided right then and there both to stop making excuses about why he couldn't achieve his own goals, and to stop accepting excuses from everyone around him. He set out on his first jog that day. Shortly thereafter, Sam met Army Major Dave Rozelle, who despite losing a leg in combat, had just completed the Iron Man triathlon. Inspired, Sam began training for endurance events.

He started with sprint triathlons, moved his way up to Olympic distance, and eventually competed in full-length Ironman triathlons consisting of a 2.4-mile swim, a 112-mile bike ride, and finally a 26.2-mile marathon. Sam spent the next few years conquering challenge after challenge. He made the national paratriathlon team three times, racing in national competitions in New York City, San Francisco, and Louisville, Kentucky. He represented team USA in two world championships in Budapest and Australia, where he was the first American paratriathlete to cross the finish line. He completed all of the North Face endurance challenges, all races of over 50 miles. He ran a marathon through White Sands, New Mexico, carrying a 35-pound pack in the Bataan Memorial Death March. He rode his bike from Oceanside, California, to Annapolis, Maryland, while competing in Race Across America (RAAM), widely considered to be the world's toughest bike race.

Sam Cila has been able to accomplish amazing things in his life. More importantly, through both his work at The Program and with various charities for wounded veterans, he has been able to positively impact the lives of thousands of people. Sam has faced more adversity than many of us will experience in a lifetime, and he continues to face it on a daily basis. He could have told himself that you can't climb mountains, or swim in the ocean, or ride a racing bike with only one hand. Instead, he attacks every challenge that life presents. He lives life to the fullest.

Nobody would fault Sam for making excuses. Instead of making them, though, he makes commitments—to be the best teammate and best team leader that he can be, on, and for, all of the teams of which he is a part.

Regardless of the adversity that we face in our own lives, we can do the same.

57

I Don't Have Enough Time

THE MOST COMMON excuse we hear is "I don't have time." There are 24 hours in day. Although we cannot change the amount of time that we have, we do choose our priorities and how we use those 24 hours to effectively address all of them. If we are saying that we don't have time to do something, we are really saying that it is not a priority for us, and/ or we didn't prepare properly to accomplish it. Therefore, complaining that we don't have time to do something is just an excuse. When we admit this to ourselves and to our teammates, we take ownership of it. If we own an issue, we have influence over it. Influence gives us control and control allows us to address and fix it.

We cannot change the amount of time that we have. We can, however, change our priorities and how we use that time.

We appreciate how busy so many readers of this book are. We are all on a lot of teams, and they all require an incredible amount of our energy and time. We also appreciate that we all have many different priorities based on a host of factors. We understand that returning a phone call, exercising, or spending meaningful time with friends and family are not the highest priorities for everyone. However, if you were to go to the gym at 4:30 a.m., for example, you would be surprised by how many people are already there working out. They are not all independently wealthy and single. They are parents and spouses. They have stressful, challenging jobs. They don't *have* the time to work out. They *make* the time to do so because it is a priority for them. The person still in bed at that early hour and the one on the treadmill both have 24 hours in their day. Working out may be a priority for both of them. The latter just prepares differently to ensure that they will address that priority at some point during those 24 hours. This is true for any of the countless things that we want to do or must accomplish in our very busy days. This is true for any priority, regardless of its place on our list of them.

We have the privilege of knowing, and working with, countless corporate employees from a hundred different industries. They have incredibly demanding schedules. However, in their 24-hour day, they exercise, call people back, file reports prior to deadlines, eat healthy, read, study, and spend time with their friends and families. They may not watch much TV, though. They don't play video games or take long lunch breaks. Admittedly, they have very little idle time in their day, unless it is by design (such as personal reflection time), but they still accomplish all their priorities. They don't have a different amount of time in their day than the rest of us; they just have different priorities and prepare accordingly to address all of them.

When our instructors at The Program are working with teams, our schedule can be demanding, to say the least. An 18-hour workday or longer is not uncommon. A typical day during our busy season may look like this:

Day 1

3 a.m.: Wake up and drive to the airport

5 a.m.: Flight

10 a.m.: Land and drive to the event

11 a.m.: Internal briefs and rehearsals

1 p.m.–9 p.m.: Day 1 of the event

9 p.m.: Dinner and internal debrief

10 p.m.: Check into hotel

11 p.m.: Sleep

Day 2

3:30 a.m.: Wake up

4:30 a.m.–12:00 p.m.: Day 2 of the event

12:00 p.m.: Drive to the airport

Repeat

We may repeat this process for a few events in a row: we leave one team and drive or fly straight to another. As you can see, there isn't much time left in the day for working out. It would be easy for our teammates to make valid excuses about why they can't stay fit. Instead, it is not unheard of for our teammates to wake up at 2 a.m. to work out before a 5 a.m. start with a team. A few years ago, Jamey Slife and another teammate were driving through the Northeast, going from event to event. Rather than take the time to find and go to a gym, they decided to pull over at a rest stop on the highway and work out. After a state trooper stopped Jamey while he ran shirtless in the breakdown lane of the highway, Jamey had the pleasure of explaining to the state trooper the priority we place on exercising as well as our belief in not making excuses.

We are all on a lot of teams. As teammates and team leaders on them, we have countless priorities. Great teammates and great team leaders do not *have* the time to address all of them. We *make* the time to do so. Or we make excuses.

58

Make Preparations, Not Excuses

IF EXCUSES ARE an admission that something wasn't a priority and/or that we failed to prepare properly to address it, it stands to reason that some prior planning could alleviate the need for excuses. We typically hear countless excuses right around mid-February. All gyms are packed on January 1. New faces abound and there is a 20-minute wait for a treadmill or a bench. By mid-February, the vast majority of those new faces will be gone and you can have your pick of open treadmills and benches. Why? Most people who set goals or resolutions fail to see them through. Most people who wake up on January 1, resolved to lose weight or save money, will not succeed. Most people will make a resolution to get in shape, but they fail to make a plan. They walk through the doors of the gym in early January with a resolution, but then spend most of their time wandering around the gym.

They do not prepare, so when mid-February rolls around and they haven't made any progress, they make excuses instead. On that first day in the gym, they may find themselves standing next to a person with as little experience as they have. However, rather than make an excuse that they had no experience, that other person has a workout plan. Maybe they downloaded it or had a knowledgeable friend write one out for them. Although they share the same initial level of experience exercising, that other person has prepared prior to beginning their workouts. That person is far more likely to see results come February and then continue to stick with it.

One of the things that we enjoy the most about working at The Program is that we don't spend much time with "most" people. We work with great leaders on football and softball fields, amazing coaches, and true visionaries in the corporate world. These individuals have no interest in being "most" people. Our teammates at The Program have no interest in being average either. They climb mountains, compete in triathlons, run 100-mile ultramarathons, and graduate from the toughest schools the Department of Defense has to offer. They have achieved, and continue to achieve, goals of which "most" people wouldn't dream.

One of the commonalties successful people share is their ability to properly prepare. Very few things in their life are left to chance. If they set a goal, they make a plan to accomplish it. Frankly, after countless false starts, we had to apply that same mindset to writing this book. At first, we went into the process with an end goal in sight, but without a real plan to get there. We would try to write during our downtime, or while in the air on cross-country flights. That approach didn't work and we made excuses about why we were not reaching our goals:

"I was barely home this month." "I didn't have Wi-Fi on my flight." "The event ran late and I didn't have time to write." And on and on.

These were all excuses and admissions that we had failed to prepare properly. When we realized this, we sat down and came up with a plan. We would make the time to write within our busy schedules. We would write a certain number of words per day and per week. We made a plan and committed to it. Preparing made it possible to write this book, instead of making excuses as to why we could not.

Sam Cila never misses workouts. He is never late for events. He is never slowed down by his missing hand. He could not do these things and would have valid excuses to offer, but Sam doesn't make excuses. Sam prepares for everything. Nothing is left to chance. His gym bag is always packed with all the gear and equipment he needs for every conceivable workout. At the airport, Sam always wears shoes with "quick laces" that he can tighten with one hand. His bag is always fastidiously packed, with his prosthetic hand easily accessible, knowing that TSA is going to freak out over it. Few people prepare as well as Sam does.

They then have to make excuses about why a TSA slowdown caused them to miss a flight, or how they didn't bring the right workout gear. Sam prepares so that he does not have to make excuses.

We all have a thousand excuses for why we don't achieve our goals in life. There is one reason: because we failed to prepare properly. There are no excuses.

59

Being Motivated Is Not Enough

COACHES AND BUSINESS leaders around the country ask us about the importance of motivation. Frankly, we don't concern ourselves with motivation. We take it as a given that the teams and corporations with whom we work already possess motivation. Motivation is *wanting* to succeed. Granted, there may be people out there who are not motivated and who do not want to succeed. If we are building a championship culture, though, we do *not* want those people around us. However, good organizations are full of people who want to succeed. There are countless "good" organizations in America. There are lots of "good" companies, schools, athletic teams, and families. We have no interest in being "good." We want to be great, and to compete for championships in everything we do. Motivation, merely *wanting* to succeed, isn't enough to compete for championships. We may desire an outcome, but without absolute commitment, we will fall short of accomplishing it.

We may desire an outcome, but without absolute commitment, we will fall short of accomplishing it.

Therefore, instead of motivation, focus on *volition* instead. Motivation is *wanting* to succeed. Volition is being absolutely committed and willing to sacrifice to do so. Everyone, including our competitors, *wants* to win. Because we (and they) want to win, we work hard. We work with enough organizations to know that while almost everyone puts in the required work to be good (because they are motivated and want to succeed), most individuals are not willing to be fully committed and to make the necessary sacrifices: they don't have the volition to be great. They aren't willing to sacrifice some of their social life so they can work on their schoolwork, their hitting technique, or practicing the guitar. Everyone wants to be a rock star in their chosen profession, but most aren't willing to sacrifice to become one.

Champions not only have the desire (motivation) to be great, but they also have the absolute commitment and willingness to sacrifice (volition) to achieve greatness. What are we motivated to accomplish? Are we completely committed and willing to sacrifice to achieve it? If not, with enough talent, we can still be good, but we will never be great.

60

We Don't Get What We Deserve—We Get What We Earn!

ONE OF THE most damaging attitudes in any organization is a sense of entitlement. When people begin to feel that they are owed something, their desire and ability to compete and attack dulls. The Program differentiates between the terms "deserve" and "earn." These terms are often used interchangeably and it drives us crazy. *Merriam-Webster* says that, "*deserve* is used when a person should rightly receive something good or bad because of his or her actions or character." The key word in that definition is "should." In a perfect world, we would get everything that we deserve. However, that is rarely the case in our imperfect world. With all the adversity that Sam Cila has faced, he deserves every accolade and achievement that has come his way. However, he did not make the National Paralympic Triathlon team because he deserved it. He made the team because he worked harder than those he beat out. Instead of making excuses about how much he deserved to be on the team, Sam earned it on his bike, in the water, and on the road during long and miserable training sessions that he didn't want to do, but that he went and did anyway.

We don't always get what we deserve, we only get what we earn. While "deserving" is a passive term involving "should," "earn" is an active word. *Merriam-Webster* says, "*earn* is used when a person has spent the time and effort to get what they deserve." Teams and

211

organizations that base their success off what they feel they deserve will always be disappointed. They may be rewarded occasionally, but "occasionally" will not allow us to compete for championships.

"We don't get what we deserve, we only get what we earn" is the mantra of a highly successful Division 1 wrestling program with whom we had the privilege to work. In practice, this meant that you could wrestle in the program for three years and win three national championships, but if you wanted a spot in the lineup your senior year, you still needed to defeat everyone else in your weight class. If the team recruited a stud freshman who then beat the senior in a wrestle-off, then that stud freshman would represent the team despite all of the hard work and accomplishments the senior earned in prior years. This may seem unfair. It is. It's a cliché, but life isn't fair. In a perfect world, we would get everything we deserved. Unfortunately, we don't live in one. It isn't about what we deserve. When we fail to accomplish our mission, we can make excuses about how unfair the process was. Or we can go and earn it.

61

Don't Let Anyone Make Excuses for You

IF WE WANT to compete for championships, we cannot make excuses. More challenging, we must never allow others to makes excuses for us either. Unfortunately, the people who love us the most (and with whom we spend the most time), tend to make the most excuses for us.

Sam Cila's loved ones could not help but make excuses for him after he had his hand amputated. They could not avoid knowing what he had been through, and they saw the pain and adversity that he experienced daily. And they made excuses. They were blinded by their love for him. At the time, Sam not only made excuses for himself about why he couldn't achieve his goals in life, but he also allowed his loved ones to make those same excuses for him. We are in no way disparaging Sam's family. We can't imagine telling a beloved child to "toughen up" after an injury like that. However, excuses only hold us back. As discussed, if we make an excuse, we are not accepting the responsibility for the outcomes in our lives. It wasn't until Sam realized this that he was able to build himself into the warrior that he is now, a warrior who is even tougher, more disciplined, and more driven than the one who joined the Army after 9/11.

However, people continue to make excuses for Sam. His mother still tries to cut his steak because, even though he is one of the toughest, most intimidating guys we know, "Poor Sammy only has one hand."

213

Sam knows those excuses come from a place of love, but he also knows that allowing them is a road back to his couch and an addiction to his pain medication. He will cut his own steak, thank you very much.

We can't make excuses for ourselves and we can't let others make them for us either. The people who love us the most often make the most excuses for us. These excuses come from a place of love, but they are still excuses. Our loved ones are not accurate evaluators of our talent, intelligence, or any other attribute. Hopefully, we have good teammates, coaches, and superiors who will tell us the truth. Our loved ones may make excuses for us; unfortunately, our competition never will. Our competition doesn't care what neighborhood we come from; they don't care that we have a cold or didn't get enough sleep last night. They don't care about any of the hardships we have faced. All our competition cares about during the heat of battle is whether we or they will accomplish the mission.

All excuses, whether they are made by us or by others on our behalf, will always stop us from reaching our potential, both as individuals and, most importantly, as members of the teams of which we are privileged to be a part. Don't allow it. Don't make excuses, and don't let others make excuses for us. Accomplish the mission!

Action Items: We Don't Make Excuses and We Don't Allow Others to Make Excuses for Us

1. Excuses hold us back from accomplishing our mission. Don't make them. Instead, focus on your preparation. If you win, continue to prepare knowing that there is someone out there who is working right now to beat you. If you lose, be that someone.
2. What are your priorities in life? This year? Today? All of our actions/behaviors should be in alignment with our priorities. Ensure that they are.
3. Figure out which people in your life make excuses for you. Do those excuses come from a good place? Most importantly, do you accept their excuses?
4. Do you make excuses for some of your teammates? Help them get better instead. Stay focused on your (and their) preparation.

Saved Round on No Excuses: One-Armed Bridge Crossing

In the Spring of 2016, we worked with a school that had an excellent ROTC facility that we were able to incorporate into our training. The ROTC facility included an "endurance course"; a trail through the woods interspersed with various obstacles. One of these obstacles was a rope bridge over a stream made from three ropes strung across it like an upside-down triangle, one rope for your feet and a rope for each hand to hold on to. All our instructors ran through the course multiple times to test the obstacles. However, a couple of them balked at the rope bridge. Mac had recently torn his bicep tendon and only had the use of one arm. Sam Cila was also limited to the use of one hand. The rope bridge was unsteady enough with the use of both hands. Both Sam and Mac looked at the rope bridge for a few minutes and then chose to climb down the bank and wade across the stream. No student-athlete or coach saw them bypass the bridge.

They made excuses why they couldn't cross the bridge. Not to others. Nobody else saw them. They made excuses for each other and to themselves. They didn't want to get hurt. They didn't want to mess up their uniforms. The rope bridge wasn't designed for one-armed use. The excuses that they made to themselves piled up and ate at them for the rest of the day. It kept them awake that night.

Sam and Mac know that you can never ask a Marine or soldier (or teammate) to do something you wouldn't do yourself (one-handed or not). Therefore, after finishing the event, debriefing with the coaches, packing away the gear, and showering, Sam and Mac jogged back out to the rope bridge and crossed it.

Don't make excuses and don't let others make excuses for you. Make a plan! Regardless of the battlefield, our preparation doesn't guarantee us winning a championship, but excuses guarantee that we never will.

SECTION
VI

Hard Work Is One More™

NEARBY, THERE WERE numerous two-story buildings with multiple entry and exit points, windows, and flat rooftops from which an enemy could fire down upon Captain Stacey Pesce and her team.

As Stacey remembers, even though she was surrounded by a team of honorable, courageous, and committed teammates, she still *felt* like a "target."

Then she and her team became one....

Captain Stacey Pesce (left) and Corporal Jennifer Hoff (right) on the morning of the Afghan National Elections.

Note: Photo courtesy of Stacey Pesce.

62

A Female Marine in Helmand Province, Afghanistan

THE PROGRAM LEAD instructor Stacey Pesce deployed to Helmand Province, Afghanistan, on April 30, 2009, as an adjutant for her unit, the 8th Engineer Support Battalion (ESB). Shortly thereafter, an Afghani woman who had been severely beaten by her husband fled to the Marines for protection. Due to cultural issues, the male Marines were limited in their ability to provide it. Instead, it was proposed to form a Female Engagement Team (FET), a team of thirty-four female Marines, made up of both officer and enlisted personnel. Their mission was to engage and influence the local populace, specifically women and children. It would be the first U.S. all-female unit to conduct combat operations in Afghanistan. A call went out to all units stationed in Afghanistan to provide female Marines for the FET. Stacey was selected as the Officer-in-Charge (OIC).

The FET exchanged information, built relationships, and provided medical care. They could breach the barriers of a highly conservative society that their male counterparts could not, enabling their team to conduct necessary searches of female civilians often covered from head to toe in a burka, helping to provide a level of security not otherwise available.

In August, the FET was tasked with supporting the Afghanistan national elections, which were being held to choose Afghanistan's next president and provincial leaders. It was an important and very contested event in Afghanistan's political and social climate. In the days and weeks leading up to it, terrorist groups carried out multiple orchestrated attacks on polling stations and city centers in attempts to disrupt the elections.

During their preparation for supporting the elections, Stacey and her Female Engagement Team received reports that the insurgency knew of their recent interaction with women and children in the local community. Remarkably, a few of these terrorist groups had been in attendance with the FET at multiple all-male shuras (community meetings) that they had attended. They saw the FET—correctly, as Stacey is quick to point out—as a threat to their own mission of keeping Afghanistan a safe home for terrorist groups. The reports concluded with a message that the enemy's main effort during the elections would be to kill or capture female Marines.

During the elections, the FET team's male Marine counterparts would not be allowed to interact with Afghan women and children for cultural reasons. Since families would be traveling to polling stations to vote, Stacey's team was divided into smaller groups at various security checkpoints near the polling stations. They set up their security checkpoint just after midnight on August 20, 2009.

63

We Work Hard

THE PROGRAM CONSIDERS working hard to be so important that it is one of the principles for success that we teach and develop (along with being physically and mentally tough, and not making excuses). Furthermore, almost every person and team believes they "work hard." "Hard work" is plastered on hundreds of motivational posters, the backs of t-shirts, and weight room walls. Every business leader discusses it with us as a hallmark of their team. However, if hard work is vitally important for success and everyone is doing it, why are there so few world-class athletic teams, companies, and cultures? We believe it is because most people do not fully understand what hard work is and are either unwilling or unable to do it.

Hard work isn't what we do during normal business hours. Hard work isn't a "normal" business day regardless of whether that "normal" is an 8-, 12-, or (for the investment banker readers of this book) 18-hour workday. Hard work isn't a "normal" 3-hour, full-contact practice, either. Both a 12-hour work day and a full-contact practice, require great effort, and we appreciate the teammates and teams who give it, but great effort is not hard work.

Hard Work Is One More™. It is our trademarked slogan. Hard work is not calculated on an absolute basis. Hard work is not necessarily a challenging summer workout for the college athlete or making thirty sales calls for the sales rep. Your competition does those things too. We consider doing what our competition is doing *giving effort*. Hard work is calculated on a relative basis. Did you outwork your competition? Did you finish your challenging workout and then do three extra sprints? Did you make your "normal" thirty cold calls and then make three more?

Hard Work Is One More™. Did you outwork your competition?

When we conduct our experiential training with teams, the consequence for not meeting a standard might be a set of challenging exercises for the team: sets of 6, 11, 16, 21, and 26. We let everyone else do sets of 5, 10, 15, 20, and 25.

When we run, we don't run to the 20-, 40-, 60-, 80-, or 100-yard line. We let our competition do that. We run to the 21-, 41-, 61-, 81-, and the 101-yard line. We do One More™.

Make One More™ a habit.

64

One More™ in a Combat Environment

STACEY PESCE IS a great teammate and leader. She stays focused on mission accomplishment first and her teammates' welfare always. Leaders demanding One More™ is for their teams' best welfare. Her Female Engagement Team made a commitment to doing One More™ throughout their training. They hoped for the best—we all should— but they prepared knowing that *the worst* was always a possibility. On the morning of August 20, 2009, that possibility happened.

It would be mission failure for the Female Engagement Team if any incident disrupted the elections. Furthermore, the FET needed to be sure that they were taking every measure possible to maximize the flow of people to cast votes. They engaged with a 30-year New York City Police Department detective, working as a contractor on a nearby forward operating base (FOB), to give insight on conducting discrete search and cordon operations in densely populated areas.

They drilled nonlethal manipulation techniques with their military police colleagues. They didn't just *give effort* during this training. They did One More™. They trained until they had carved huge divots in the dirt and sand from the number of times they fell and grappled.

They demanded issuance of, and training for, the Marine Corps' most advanced remote detonation device jammer to aid in avoiding being blown up by a terrorist using a cell phone. They knew other operational units had this tool, and they exploited every point of contact they had to obtain one for themselves.

Their medic, also a woman, drilled every member of the FET on battlefield lifesaving techniques from applying tourniquets to running intravenous (IV) fluids. They did these drills until every member of the team could meet her exacting standard of triage proficiency. Then, she pulled out her stopwatch and made every member of the team achieve the same standard of proficiency, but faster. Then, they were blindfolded in order to ensure that those same standards could be met, literally, "with their eyes closed."

Fatigue meant a lack of energy to accomplish their mission, as well as a lack of energy to give to both their FET Marine teammates and the Afghani people—specifically the women and children they were sworn to protect. They had to ensure that they did everything they could to ensure that didn't happen. Normal daily workouts, as well as martial arts training, were conducted wearing full combat loads (an additional 30–50 pounds), to ensure that all members of the FET could not only maneuver between various polling locations, but could then remain on their feet upon arrival for 10-, 12-, or 14-hour days. Their physical training standard was not to simply accomplish these tasks, but to do them without fatigue, knowing that it would lead to a deterioration in their physical, mental, and emotional capabilities—a killer on any battlefield (and at home and in the office as well).

Furthermore, they fabricated elaborate election scenarios, bought burkas at the local market, and did full-dress rehearsals of their immediate actions in case of an incident. They asked both male and female colleagues to be "actors" in these scenarios. They didn't just draw it out on a whiteboard or go through the motions of rehearsing. They made the scenarios as "real" as they possibly could.

65

Long-Term Greedy

THE VENERABLE FINANCIAL institution Goldman Sachs teaches its new hires: "Never make a short-term financial decision at the expense of long-term wealth creation." For your client, or yourself, be "long-term greedy."

There are numerous factors that determine The Program's decisions. First, is the decision in line with our Core Values? Second, will it help us accomplish our mission? Finally, we may call a trusted mentor or, at the very least, think about what an influential person in our lives would do or suggest to us. All these factors influence our decision-making process. However, when faced with a tough decision, the *long-term greedy* answer is the correct one. Stacey Pesce wanted to be nice to her Female Engagement Team and not train the extra hours that she and their mission demanded. Those extra hours were long-term greedy, though.

I want ice cream for dessert most nights. Should I have it?

I want to buy my children the toys they ask for every time we go shopping. Do I buy them?

I don't want to work out. I want to take today off. Not working out means that I have an easier day—I won't experience discomfort. Should I stay sitting on the couch?

I want to golf today. I want to go out tonight. I don't want to study/ work. I'm tired. Does the extra studying/work that I could do really make that big a difference?

Happiness is internal. It is a state of mind. We remain happy regardless of the presence or absence of external factors. Happiness is long-lived. Pleasure is dependent on external factors. We have a feeling of pleasure only for as long as the external factor lasts. It is momentary.[1]

Like the first two little pigs, we might be able to have more *pleasure* now if we make decisions based on our desire for it, but we must remember that pleasure is short lived. Eventually, a big, bad wolf (or a terrorist group, a bad economy, or an injury to our starting quarterback) will come and blow our house (or life) down. That will not make us *happy*.

In Goldman Sachs terms, the short-term, "easy" decision may give us more pleasure, but it almost never makes us long-term happy. We derive pleasure from a bowl of ice cream, but the ability to play with our kids makes us happy. Watching more TV gives us pleasure. A workout during that time provides us with more energy to devote to stronger, healthier relationships with co-workers and family members. That makes us happy. Easy days spent lounging by the pool gives us pleasure, but a long, tough, challenging commitment to, and achievement of, a personal or team goal makes us happy.

This is not to say that we should never eat that bowl of ice cream or take a day off from work or studying, but rather to ask yourself prior to doing so whether this is a short-term, pleasure-driven decision, or whether it will make you happy. Stacey and her FET teammates consistently chose happiness. More free time to relax while in Afghanistan would give them pleasure. However, the long-term greedy decision was a commitment to an incredible amount of hard work, to doing One More™. It would allow them to return safely to family members and friends upon completion of their deployment. That would make them happy.

Instead of doing things that only give you pleasure, be long-term greedy. It will make you happy. One More™ is that commitment.

---

[1] "Difference Between Happiness and Pleasure," https://www.differencebetween .com/difference-between-happiness-and-vs-pleasure/, April 8, 2015.

66

Focus on Strengths, Address Weaknesses

SUPPORTING THE ELECTIONS in Afghanistan would be the biggest, most dynamic, and high-profile mission that Stacey and the FET had been on up until that time. There was not, however, any precedent for what supporting a politically charged, volatile national election might entail. They weren't given a handbook that laid out all the training the FET should conduct in order to be successful at their assigned mission. Despite the uncertainty, the FET charged forward knowing their strengths and their weaknesses. They focused on their strengths in order to maximize their use when an enemy appeared. A weakness may never become a strength, especially in the short term, and if more talent is required. We are all talented at certain things and not talented at others. Our weaknesses must still be addressed, though. Stacey and her FET teammates addressed their weaknesses daily to ensure that when the enemy appeared, at the very least, those weaknesses could not, and would not, be exploited.

We all have strengths on which we must focus to ensure that we can use them to their utmost in accomplishing our mission. We also all have a vulnerability, a weakness in our game or our personality that can hurt our ability to be the most successful individuals and teams on our chosen battlefields. We all have that *something* that, if improved, will make us a better athlete, salesperson, doctor, director of HR, or marketing or customer service rep—something that will make us a better parent, a better teammate, a better team leader. We should focus on our strengths, but address weaknesses too. Like Stacey and her FET teammates, it will allow us to accomplish our own missions.

Determine Our One More™

Write down one thing that you do well that helps the team win. Then write down one thing that, if addressed, would help the team win even more. Author Simon Sinek calls a version of this a Team Effectiveness Exercise. We call it "A Way to Determine Our One More." Try not to think about it as a strength and a weakness. Think about it as something you already do that helps the team win and then something that, if addressed, would help the team win even more. Ask a teammate to do the same for you. The teammate can be our spouse, partner, athletic teammate, coach, CEO, friend, or mentor. The more teammates we can get to do it for us, the better. Tendencies will start to appear.

Keep feedback focused on behaviors rather than on a talent or performance. For example, "Your work ethic is the best of anyone on the team," rather than "You are always our number one salesperson." For areas of improvement, "You need to be more emotionally resilient; you react emotionally, rather than passionately." Highlighting this behavior is more impactful than the performance to which it leads: "You get too many technical fouls." Focus on areas that are choices for ourselves and for teammates.

The Program's "A Way to Determine Our One More" can be conducted in a group setting or individually.

Compounding Our Choice to Do One More™

Once we have determined the behavior that, if addressed, would help our team accomplish its mission better, more efficiently, more easily, or with greater frequency, we must then decide how much time of each day we devote to it. One hour? Two? More? We recommend eleven minutes. Devote eleven minutes every single day to doing that thing that, if addressed, would help us and/or our team to win more, to do better. Unfortunately, we will not see a difference tomorrow, or next week. That isn't the way our lives work.

We all want instant gratification. That's normal. Its occurrence is not! As Darren Hardy points out in *The Compound Effect*, if offered either $3 million today or a penny compounded for a thirty-one-day month, almost everyone would choose the $3 million. Unfortunately, that isn't the way our lives work. We aren't given $3 million (or at least most of us aren't). We want instant gratification, but we don't get it. Instead, we get pennies. A penny represents a good or bad decision in every aspect of our lives.

In this example, our initial penny will be good decisions, but our bad decisions *compound* just as effectively. One "good" penny becomes two pennies on Day 2. It becomes four pennies on Day 3 and eight pennies on Day 4. After a week, that penny is worth 64 cents. After two weeks, our good decisions have compounded to be worth $81.92. This is the time when most people stop making good decisions. If we make good decisions, after two weeks, we only have $81.92 and we compare ourselves to our teammate or neighbor, whom we perceive to have $3 million. We get frustrated, disappointed, or discouraged and we stop making those good decisions.

However, if we instead choose to focus on making good decisions rather than on outcomes or what we think our neighbors have, then after twenty-nine days, we have $2.5 million. It still is not as much as the $3 million, but close. On the thirtieth day though, our good decisions have compounded to $5 million! On the thirty-first day, they are worth $10 million.

Rest assured that on the thirty-first day, after choosing to make hundreds or thousands of daily *good* decisions, sacrificing, doing One More™, we will wake up in the morning and everyone will tell us how *lucky* we are. Success has very little to do with luck, though. Thinking it does is just the way others cope with their own lack of discipline and unwillingness to make those same thousands of good decisions— their unwillingness to committing to One More™.

One More™ has nothing to do with luck or talent. One More™ is a choice. Make better choices. Focus on strengths. Address weaknesses. And commit to doing so for a very long time. Great choices, like pennies, add up, and produce great achievements.

67

Determining Our "Why"

As INDIVIDUALS, IT is incredibly important to figure out what drives us. We need to find out, as Simon Sinek famously wrote, what our "why" is. Why do we wake up in the morning? Why do we do what we do? We enjoy Simon's books and are big fans of *Start with Why: How Great Leaders Inspire Everyone to Take Action*. We just don't necessarily agree with its initial premise, as we have highlighted here in this book. Instead, we must start with *who*. We must ensure that the people in our organizations share our Core Values. Combined with talent, they form the foundation of a world-class culture. Once that has been established though, the *why* is powerful and of vital importance.

The FET is a wonderful reflection of this. Although both often occur, the Marine Corps does not entice or recruit its members with promises of their receiving a college education or an opportunity to see the world. Instead, the Marine Corps states that their Core Values are Honor, Courage, and Commitment. They define each and have incredibly high standards to reinforce each daily. The Marine Corps' mission, their *why*, is to defend the people of the United States at home and abroad, to fight our nation's battles swiftly and aggressively in times of crisis.

Although the Marine Corps does not promise a college education or an opportunity to see the world, it does promise its members a *what* if the recruit shares the *who* and the *why* of the Marine Corps (and can graduate from Officer Candidate School or Marine Corps boot camp): the opportunity to call themselves Marines.

In Afghanistan, the FET Marines had to continue to fulfill all tasks and responsibilities in their current primary units, while also conducting all the FET's additional combat operations. They were paid no extra money and they would be operating in an extremely volatile and deadly environment. Marines had to volunteer to be a member of the FET.

There were more volunteers than there were spots on the team.

Stacey and her teammates were Marines. They were honorable, courageous, and committed. To assist the Marine Corps in accomplishing its mission, they were tasked with engaging and influencing the local populace, specifically to protect the women and children of Afghanistan. This was their mission, their *why*. It was also the personal mission of all its individual members. They shared the FET's Core Values and its *why*.

Recently when working with an NFL team, we met with their leadership counsel. The meeting began with a simple question from us to the athletes: "Why do you do what you do?" Each player had to explain *why* he played football. These are all professional athletes competing at the highest levels, all from very different backgrounds. Almost all athletes answered the question exactly as every other high-performing person and team has answered: passion.

Not all of us are passionate about what we do in our daily lives and, in fact, many of us don't even generally like what we are doing. We are almost all passionate about something, though. Stay focused on it! That is your *why*. We may not be passionate about our job, but we are passionate about the family that it allows us to support, and the better we do at that job, the better we do in supporting what we are passionate about—our *why*.

We may not all be passionate about what we do, but almost all of us are passionate about something. Stay focused on it!

In order to compete for championships, on any battlefield, we must have something that drives us. There must be something that makes us want to get up early in the morning and then stay later than our competitors. When our goals are rooted in, and backed by, true passion (our *why*) it is amazing what we can achieve. As leaders, we have a responsibility to develop our people. But we can do so only if they have an individual drive, a "care factor", that pushes them to better themselves. Leaders can inspire. Motivation, though, is an internal desire or drive. Leaders aren't internal. We can't motivate. Thankfully, we don't need to; our team members' individual *whys* can!

Unfortunately, numerous individuals and teams don't have a *why*, or at least not a very strong one. We work with numerous college and professional athletes, as well as CEOs, whose *why* is more about the ancillary benefits of being a college athlete or CEO of a major corporation than it is about bettering themselves or their team. Unfortunately, in times of great adversity, the moments that determine the great teams from the merely good, the ancillary benefits of our positions—the free shoes and the business perks—are quickly forgotten. We love those benefits when things are going well, but those benefits aren't present in the middle of a summer training session, or at one o'clock in the morning when a valued member of our executive team needs help.

An All-Pro free safety with whom we work spoke about his *why*—specifically, his love for the game. He talked about how he loved the preparation, he loved the grind. He loved running sprints, watching film, lifting weights, and attacking drills. He has a true passion for the game and everything that goes with it. He still may not like a 5 a.m. alarm, but it is easier for him to answer that bell than someone whose *why* is the screaming of 100,000 fans. There aren't any at 5 a.m.

Examine your own *why*. What drives you to do the things you do? Even without a strong *why*, we can be still be good at something. Our talent affords us that ability. We will just never be great.

Finally, as a leader, make it a priority to know the "whys" of your teammates. Knowing what truly drives and motivates teammates will allow us to tailor our messaging and provide appropriate benefits to inspire them to achieve their best.

68

The FET Is a Target

As soon as the sun came up that morning, people began arriving at the FET's checkpoint. All vehicles entering the area near the polling station were searched. Women and children were removed from the vehicles and directed over to Stacey's team, where they could be searched for weapons or explosives behind a privacy barrier.

After Stacey and her team had been on their feet and engaged in this incredibly physically and mentally tough and tense environment for more than ten hours, a dingy and rusted vehicle drove up. An Afghan woman and man got out. When directed over to Stacey and her team, the man grabbed the woman by the elbow and with one arm around her waist, began to push her in Stacey's direction. She was covered from head to toe in a blue burka. All the other women up until that moment had come over to the FET's location without being accompanied by any men.

Stacey could tell immediately that something was "not right." The woman was fidgeting, dragging her feet, and had to be forcibly moved forward by her male companion. Stacey recalls her heart beating so hard that she felt like it was lifting and lowering the entire vest of body armor she was wearing. As a sign of cultural respect, she and her teammates wore headscarves under their Kevlar helmets to hide their necks and hair. Stacey was so scared, she felt like the head scarf was strangling her. Her tongue felt like a giant wad of dry cotton stuck to the roof of her mouth. She thought this was it. This was their enemy, making good on their earlier threat.

233

As the officer in charge, she had difficult decisions to make and only seconds to make them. The mission and the safety of every single one of her FET teammates—sisters, daughters, wives, and mothers—depended on those decisions that Stacey would have to make in the next few seconds.

Immediately, Stacey shouted at the woman and demanded that she stop and lift her burka. The man just kept shoving her forward. Despite the Female Engagement Team's weapons now pointed at her, the woman (and her male companion) continued toward them.

Should she give her FET teammates the order to fire?! If given now, they would be at a distance where any blast from an explosive device being worn by the woman might injure them but not kill them or anyone else at the polling station. But that order would have to be given right now!

Stacey and her FET teammates fell back on their training and the habits developed during their thousands of hours of hard work, of doing One More™. It helped provide her with the intuition to order her teammates not to shoot, to hold their fire. Instead, she decided on a different course of action. She instructed one of her FET teammates, Corporal Jennifer Hoff, to immediately approach the woman and her male companion and conduct the search. The entire rest of the team would provide security for her. In order for Corporal Hoff to do her job though, she would be dangerously close to the woman. She would undoubtedly die if the woman blew herself up. Stacey's teammate had received and understood the same earlier reports threatening the FET team. Would Corporal Hoff execute Stacey's order?

Should Stacey do the search herself? The FET had seen Stacey conduct searches before, so they, and Corporal Hoff, knew that she could. What would happen in the time it took Stacey to run up to the woman's position? What was best for her team? Stacey and her FET teammates were located at multiple polling locations. If there was violence to follow, Stacey was responsible for getting her entire team to safety. Based on the threatening report they had been given, the violent events in the time leading up to the elections, and the unusual behavior of this Afghan woman, they had enough information for fear to present itself. Stacey still felt that they did not have enough information to pull a trigger.

Consistent behavior during thousands of hours of hard work, of One Mores™, had helped develop an incredible level of trust throughout the entire Female Engagement Team—trust that each member of the team would do their job when called upon. She told her teammate to move forward and conduct the search. Without hesitation, Corporal Hoff moved forward. Under all the layers of this Afghan woman's clothing, in the over 100-degree heat, she wasn't strapped with an explosive device as they had thought. She was holding her limp and near-lifeless infant in her arms. Stacey's heart cried in sympathy for that Afghani woman and her young son.

She was struck with a wave of emotions thinking about her decision not to fire, an action that she and her team were dangerously close to doing, and what the devastating consequences would have been had they done so. Stacey wasn't to become a mother for another eight years, but she inherently knew that the most innocent and precious thing in this world was being cradled in the arms of that woman.

If Stacey and her teammates had let fear take over, and not followed the rules of engagement, they would have killed an innocent Afghan woman, possibly her infant son, and completely derailed the Afghan national elections. If they had kept a fearful distance from the woman, failed to search her, and allowed her to pass through the checkpoint while possibly carrying an explosive device, they could have hurt or killed their teammates on the other side of the checkpoint and numerous innocent civilians.

Stacey and her team had been up all night long and had already performed hundreds of searches. The heat was brutal. Complacency was an ever-present threat. Physically, mentally, and emotionally, it was a huge contradiction for Stacey to point her weapon at another woman. More crippling was the moral battle she fought inside herself about asking her teammate, Corporal Hoff, to move forward and conduct a search that could severely injure or most probably kill her. The decision-making and subsequent execution of those decisions that day was physical, mental, and emotional hard work.

Stacey and her team were able to do that hard work because of the commitment to hard work, to One More™ that they had made well before that adversity struck. They always *hoped* for the best, but did One More™ *expecting* the worst.

In preparation, Stacey knew that if they didn't hold each other accountable to doing One More™ (one more search scenario, one more casualty evacuation drill, one more weapons systems check, one more brutally intense workout), then there might be at least one day during their deployment that the enemy would hold them accountable for not doing so. Stacey and her FET teammates ensured that this would not occur, and because of it, rather than take a life on the morning of August 20, 2009, they saved one—that of a nine-month-old baby boy.

Action Items on Hard Work

As the saying goes, "There is no substitute for hard work." We agree. Unfortunately, most people don't appreciate or understand what hard work is.

1. Hard work is not calculated on an absolute basis. Hard work is calculated on a relative basis. Did you outwork your competition? Hard Work Is One More™. If "normal" is thirty sales calls, do it and then make three more.
2. **Throughout our lives, we should never make short-term decisions that might give pleasure at the cost of long-term decisions that will provide us with happiness.** Think of those things that make us truly happy and then ensure that all our short-term decisions are in line with our achieving them. Be long-term greedy.
3. Our competition will always exploit our weaknesses. To combat this, we need to focus on our strengths, but continuously work on improving our deficiencies—in all aspects of our lives.

Saved Round on Hard Work: Because I Said So

Contrary to many people's misguided perception, when an officer in the military yells "Jump," their subordinates do not automatically respond with "How high?" In fact, until an incredible level of trust has been developed (and even at times after that), subordinates will ask, "Why?" When this occurs in the middle of a game, during a critical juncture of a business meeting, or during a combat operation though, the effects can be detrimental to mission accomplishment at best and life threatening at worst.

When Corporal Hoff was told to "jump," she jumped! Immediately and without hesitation. If we want our subordinates to behave like Corporal Hoff on our own battlefields, as parents, teachers, coaches, business leaders, and yes, even officers in the military, when asked why, though our overwhelming emotional desire may be to respond with "Because I said so," don't. Instead, if we take the time, whenever possible, to thoughtfully respond and provide meaningful information to our subordinates in response to their asking *why* (or even better, we provide it at the outset so they don't need to ask), although teammates may still dislike what is being asked of them, they will do it knowing that there is a purpose behind it that will help the team accomplish its mission. If we don't have a good answer and our only response to why is "Because I said so," your athlete, corporate employee, or child is right and there is no reason for your assigned task to be accomplished. If something isn't helping us to accomplish our mission, we shouldn't do it, regardless of the battlefield.

SECTION

VII

Effective Communication

Lieutenant Commander Ghislane Stonnaker (left) and Lieutenant Commander David Hunt (right) signal to aircraft pilots on a ship's flight deck.

Note: Photo courtesy of Ghislaine Stonnaker, Lt. Cmdr. (Ret).

69

Alone on the Beach

THE PREVIOUS CHAPTERS have explained what a championship culture is, who great team teammates and great team leaders are within that culture, and how they prepare in order to fill either role. However, without an ability to communicate, our efficacy as both great teammates and great team leaders will be severely limited. Poor communication is one of the most glaring signs of an ineffective and underperforming team. By the same token, great communication is one of the hallmarks of championship-caliber organizations. We appreciate that the toughest thing two people can do is communicate. Mission accomplishment almost always depends on it, though. In the photo appearing on the first page of this section, The Program teammate Ghislaine Stonnaker is using hand and arm signals to communicate with aircraft pilots on the flight deck of a ship. Miscommunication there will have very serious consequences. The same is true in our own daily lives, on all the teams of which we are privileged to be a part.

Mission accomplishment depends on our ability to communicate.

241

A few years ago, Mac had the honor of listening to a World War II veteran speak about his experiences on D-Day in Normandy. The older veteran spoke hauntingly about coming ashore in one of the early waves. The first few waves sustained massive casualties and were pinned down by German machine-gun fire. This soldier spoke about the death and destruction occurring all around him. Every man found his own hole or ditch on the beach and threw himself down in it. Momentum stopped. He related that the individual soldiers with him withdrew into themselves and they stopped communicating. Even though thousands of soldiers were on the beach with him, he felt alone. Not until sergeants forced him and his fellow soldiers to move, and the men began to communicate, did that feeling subside. Subsequently, they were able to attack as a team.

Regardless of the battlefield, we see a very similar phenomenon occur. During an athletic competition, a team is hit with some form of adversity and communication ceases. Maybe they make a costly error, a teammate is injured, or the other team goes on a ten-point run. The athletes' focus turns internal, they stop communicating with one another, and, because of it, they are unable to play as a team. Performance continues to deteriorate. You can always come back after the other team scores a touchdown. It is very difficult after they score three straight. A lack of communication allows it.

This happens in corporations as well. If adversity hits and communication ceases, cooperation and cohesion suffer. Sections no longer work toward accomplishing the organization's mission, but rather focus on their own needs and desires. Jealousies, misunderstandings, and friction flare up and interdepartmental rivalries become more important than the success of the organization.

Thankfully, we don't stop communicating because of adversity. Adversity occurs and we don't know how or what to communicate. This section will cover both.

70

Using CLAPP to Communicate Effectively

THERE IS A big difference between talking and communicating. At The Program, we don't try to change the way anyone talks. When you are spending time with friends, teammates, or co-workers, talk how you talk. Based on numerous factors, we all may talk differently; we may have different accents or use different slang. However, when we are "communicating" information, whether during a staff meeting, a time out, or a mission brief, there are very specific ways in which we do so.

CLAPP is how we communicate effectively. It stands for Clear, Loud, with Authority, Pauses, and good Posture.

Clear: We can say all the right things, but if it isn't received by our intended audience, it does us no good. Speaking clearly is paramount to ensuring that all our information is received. Many people mumble. Don't. Annunciate your words. What may seem an appropriate tempo in our heads often is spoken much too quickly for our audience to understand, especially if speaking with a microphone. Speak more slowly than you think you should.

243

Loud: Speak at the appropriate volume. For most people, this means, speak loudly. Not only will this ensure that everyone hears what you are saying, but it displays confidence in your messaging as well. Of course, "loud" is relative. Speaking loudly in a small conference room may mean that your volume is barely above that of your normal voice. Speaking loudly on the goal line in Memorial Stadium in Lincoln, Nebraska, with 90,000 screaming fans, may require every bit of volume and energy you can muster.

Furthermore, always be aware of your body position and its relation to the audience. If facing your audience, you may be using an appropriate volume. However, if you turn to face another side of the room, you will need to communicate louder.

Finally, be aware of the entire audience. Often, someone in the front of a room asks a question, and although the leader's volume while responding may be appropriate for the individual who asked the question, no one else in the room is able to hear the answer. Use the appropriate volume for the member of the audience furthest away from you.

Authority: In stressful, chaotic, adverse environments, we don't have time for "fluff." Tell people what you need them to do. We don't need to preface our statements with "If it's not too much trouble," or "If you don't mind." These modifiers waste time and make you appear less confident in your messaging. If you have proven yourself to be a good teammate and leader through your words and actions, telling your teammates authoritatively what you need them to do will not be received negatively. Speaking with authority does not mean yelling orders; it means that we should speak as if we are a subject matter expert.

Pause: Although it may feel awkward, inserting pauses into your speaking cadence allows your audience to keep up. It will also allow you to properly formulate your next thought before speaking. It is important that these be actual pauses and not just fillers. Using "like," "umm," or "know what I'm saying?" after every other sentence is distracting to the audience and will ruin the clarity of your messaging. Pausing will also automatically slow us down and help us communicate more clearly.

Posture: Much of our communication is nonverbal. Weak body language and poor posture can ruin confidence. You can say all the right things and yet be betrayed by your body language. We are visual beings. If you think that you are "doing great," but visually the audience feels that your body language is telling a different story, then as far as the audience is concerned, you are not doing great. There are many intricacies of body language, but the easiest one to address is posture. Before you communicate, make a conscious effort to stand tall and pull your shoulders back. If you are not a naturally confident speaker, keep your chin up, and your shoulders back. Uncross your arms. Like magic, you will become more confident.

For most of us, it may not be realistic to be great at all these things right away. Pick one to improve upon. For example, focus on being loud if that is your weakest area of communicating. Once you can communicate louder, work on your clarity or authority.

Similarly, when you are trying to improve the communication of your teammates and subordinates, do not expect them to improve all the facets of CLAPP simultaneously. If a teammate needs to be louder, focus on that alone. Do not also try to fix their clarity or posture simultaneously with their volume; just focus on getting them to communicate louder. A way to develop this would be to force them to deliver any messaging from ten, fifteen, or even twenty feet away from their audience.

Mac learned the true importance of effective communication during the initial invasion of Iraq while in charge of a light armored reconnaissance platoon. Each vehicle commander wears a helmet that can send and receive radio traffic. It allows them to communicate internally with the crew; tell the driver where to go, and the gunner where and what to shoot. They also have two radio channels they can use. Typically, one channel is used to communicate with the vehicles in their unit, while the second channel is used to communicate with other forces. The vehicle commander can choose with whom to communicate; however, he needs to listen to *all* the channels simultaneously. In the span of thirty seconds, he may need to tell his gunner to engage a target over the intercom, issue commands to his other vehicles on one channel, and give a situation report to his boss on another.

When the invasion kicked off, the radios were a constant flood of voices. In addition, every time anyone in the area received any type of incoming enemy rocket or mortar rounds, everyone had to don their gas masks, sometimes for hours at a time. This meant that any communication over the radio was like trying to talk on the phone with a pillow over your face. This was the most challenging environment Mac had ever had to communicate in. Effective communication wasn't a luxury, but an absolute life-or-death necessity.

The stakes in Iraq may have been different, but the principles are the same for all of us. Effective communication is the hallmark of a successful leader and organization. Focusing on CLAPP and communicating Clearly, Loudly, with Authority, Pauses, and good Posture helps all of us to accomplish the mission, regardless of the battlefield.

71

Listening to Understand

As DISCUSSED, THE Program teammate Jamey Slife was hand-selected for Marine Corps Special Operations Command Detachment One (MC SOCOM Det 1). To prepare for a combat deployment to the Middle East, Jamey and his teammates went through an intense seven-month training cycle. It was during this training that Jamey learned something that has impacted his life ever since, and it had nothing to do with shooting, fighting, or blowing stuff up.

In order to be successful in combat, Det 1 needed to train to an elite standard in Close Quarter Battle (CQB) tactics. Close Quarter Battle is when we go into a house or building, often filled with bad guys. Essentially, it is the military version of SWAT. Jamey's unit started their four-week CQB training session and had hired outside help; his name was Larry. Larry would be training them on advanced tactics "tried and true" from combat experience inside of an elite unit. Jamey's unit was an extremely regimented organization and had been trained to do things one way. Larry saw their way of doing things and he attempted to change them. He had a conversation with their entire team. The conversation started off with Larry's reasons on why he wanted to change their methods and tactics. Jamey's leadership was very quick to defend and argue why they could not adopt a new concept. The conversation became more intense, and finally Larry said something that no one was expecting him to say. He looked around at Jamey and his teammates, paused, and then said, "Fine, don't do what I am telling you. You hired me, and I get paid regardless of whether I train you or not. I will sit over here for the next two weeks and collect the paycheck, but look around. Decide which three of you are not coming home after your deployment. Decide which three of you are willing to die for your tactics." Larry then walked off.

What did Jamey learn in that critical moment? We must listen to *understand*, instead of listening to *respond*. At that moment, Jamey realized that in most of the conversations we find ourselves in, we are listening to respond and not listening to understand. Too many times, we find ourselves hearing words coming out of someone's mouth and are waiting for them to stop talking so we can give an answer, advice, or rebuttal. We are listening to respond to what they are saying rather than listening to understand what they are saying.

We must listen to understand *rather than listen to respond.*

Our ability to communicate effectively is often determined by our ability to listen. Specifically, our ability to listen to *understand*. Listening to understand when in a heated conversation or argument is very challenging. However, if we can take a moment to listen to what is being said, process the information, understand it, and the speaker, most of the time, we will diffuse the situation and build trust with the person with whom we are engaging. This does not mean we have to agree all the time. We are simply showing that we did hear them and that we understand what they are saying.

Ryan Steele, the manager of the Lowes Miami Beach Hotel, reinforced how important empathy and listening to understand are to the success of his team. On a near daily basis he may have uncomfortable conversations with both his team and clients. During these conversations, he always restates the other person's concerns or asks follow-on questions to demonstrate that he is truly empathetic to their concerns and is doing his absolute best to address and fix them. This process of listening to understand allows Ryan to provide the mentorship to his teammates, and exceptional level of customer service to his clients,that his company and property are known for.

Larry changed Jamey and his teammates' way of thinking and they changed their tactics. Jamey and his teammates deployed for seven months and they brought everyone home. Unfortunately, we don't all have the "Larry" in our lives who can throw something out there that will stop us in our tracks, cut us deep, and force us to reconsider our perspective. Instead, we must make a habit to listen to *understand*. Start now. Listen to your significant other, sibling, co-worker, or teammate. Understand what he or she is saying. Listening to understand is a vital part of our ability to effectively communicate, and will help us to become a better parent, co-worker, mentor, coach, teammate, or CEO.

72

Battlefield Communication

BATTLEFIELD COMMUNICATION IS incredibly important for athletes, coaches, and members of our armed forces and first-responder communities. We believe it is just as important for teachers and anyone who works with young people. It is equally important for those who experience chaos, in any form, in their chosen profession, as well as in our most important role as parent and spouse.

Communication becomes most difficult when we are on a battlefield. When bullets are snapping by your head, or a surging crowd is clamoring and screaming, communicating with your teammates is formidable, but also paramount to our success. Words can get drowned out and our attention can be snatched by something else more pressing. We further complicate the environment when we do not communicate effectively. Too often, in a fit of frustration, people will yell a general statement, to no one in particular. "We have to work harder!" or "Catch the ball!" The impact on the team is no different from the drunk, shirtless, painted fan in the stands yelling "Play defense!" Nobody listens to that guy either.

Battlefield communication has three components: name, command, and volume.

Name: Use your teammate's name. Yelling "Let's go guys" has never worked. It doesn't work in the office, on the basketball court, or during a firefight. Direct your message to the person who needs to hear it. We all like to hear our name called and are far more likely to pay attention to the message delivered when our name is used.

Command: Tell your teammates what you need them to do. During the heat of battle, literal or figurative, we don't have time to be unsure and insecure. Using modifiers like "I think" or "maybe" only dilutes the message. Be clear with your command and communication.

Volume: Use the volume appropriate for the location and situation. For a pair of Marine Corps Scout Snipers in a hide site executing a reconnaissance and surveillance mission, the appropriate volume may be a whisper. On a volleyball court, football field, pool deck, or trading floor, the appropriate volume is nearly always *loud!*

Say the person's name, give the command, and use the right volume. Make it a habit. This isn't the way we naturally talk though. We deliver the command before we ever use the person's name. During Thanksgiving dinner you may hear someone say, "Please pass the mashed potatoes, Mom." Very rarely will you hear "Mom! Please pass the mashed potatoes to your right." This is all well and good when we are *talking* at the dinner table, but the problem is that, quite often, especially in the chaotic environment of a battlefield, we don't start listening until we hear our name.

Mac attended a football practice of one of our FBS clients recently. During a scrimmage against the offense, one of the defensive backs walked up too close to the line of scrimmage. Before the snap, the free safety yelled, "Quarters!" wanting his teammate to switch his coverage responsibilities and back up off the line. When he didn't receive a response, he yelled "Quarters!!" even louder. He continued screaming "Quarters!" with increasing volume, intensity, and frustration until the ball was snapped. The defensive back was still lined up incorrectly and the defense gave up a big play to the offense. When the coach ran over to the Safety, the player said exasperatedly, "Coach, I yelled "Quarters."" It was clear that the defensive back who had walked up too close to the line of scrimmage was so focused on his task that he never heard the command from the safety. The coach covered the concept of name, command, and volume with both of his players. A few days later, the same situation presented itself on the game field, only this time nearly 90,000 fans screamed themselves hoarse. This time the Safety first yelled his teammate's name to get his attention, then gave him the command "Quarters!" and also used the appropriate volume, which in this case was to yell as loud as he possibly could. This time, the defense was in perfect position and shut the other team down.

73

Three Important Questions

BATTLEFIELD COMMUNICATION IS incredibly important to athletes, coaches, and members of our military and first responder communities on their battlefields. These three questions are vitally important for our success in the corporate one.

Communication is the bridge that links our teammates. Great organizations make it a habit to *overcommunicate*. If CLAPP forms the basis of *how* we communicate, the question still remains as to *what* we communicate. As a young lieutenant in the Marine Corps, Mac's commanding officer made the platoon commanders place a sign on their desks with three questions on it. Great teammates and great team leaders answer these three questions every day. Breakdowns in communication occur when we fail to consistently ask, answer, and follow through on each. These questions are:

1. What do I know?
2. Who else needs to know it?
3. Have I told them?

What do I know? What information do I possess from interactions with superiors, peers, subordinates, clients, prospects, or our competition that will help our team accomplish its mission? Do my teammates also know this information?

Who else needs to know it? Who else on my team will also benefit from knowing what I know? Is there a reason for me not to share it with the entire team? Should I only tell my superiors or those in a position of authority? Is there a reason for me not to tell my superiors? Is this something that can, and should be, addressed with my peers and subordinates? Am I absolutely sure that this is the case?

Have I told them? Is this information mission critical? Do I need to share it right away or can it wait for our weekly meeting? Would I bet my career on my ability to effectively prioritize its importance? Am I assuming, or is there a reason for me to assume, that my team already knows it? Have I already explicitly shared the information with my teammates and is there a reason for me not to reiterate it to them? What assumptions or excuses am I making for not communicating this information to them?

Attempting to answer all of these questions is incredibly time-consuming and energy draining. Often, when we do so, we can't answer all of them with 100% certainty, so we choose to answer none of them. Instead, we talk ourselves into believing that we don't know anything (which, by the way, is "something" and absolutely can, and should be, communicated), it is unimportant, nobody else really needs to know it, and therefore there is no need to say anything. We "put our head down" and just *do our job*. Remember, our job is not only to dribble, pass, or shoot. Our job is not just to do the tasks associated with our job title. Our job is to be a great teammate and a great team leader. To be great, we must effectively communicate. As former University of Miami Hurricane Head Coach, and current Detroit Lion Defensive Line Coach, Al Golden says, "In the absence of communication, there is the unknown, there is darkness. And we are severely limited in what we can do in it!"

When we fail to communicate effectively, regardless of the reasons (read: *excuses*), our team is "in the dark," and it inevitably leads to a breakdown in unit cohesion and mission failure. Don't allow it!

Stay fanatically focused in answering three simple questions: What do I know? Who else needs to know it? Have I told them?

Ask these three questions every day and overcommunicate your answers to them throughout your entire organization. Great teammates and great team leaders do, and it helps ensure great unit cohesion and, ultimately, the accomplishment of our missions that are so dependent on it.

74

Tell Your Teammates What You Want Them to Do!

IN TIMES OF stress, it is incredibly challenging for us to process negative communication. During adverse situations, our brain is often unable to process all the sensory input it is receiving. This is called "auditory exclusion." It often leads to poor or inconsistent hearing. In a military or athletic scenario, negative communication means we may say, "Don't shoot," "Don't pass," or "Don't call time out." In corporate environments, a pharmaceutical company may suffer an unsuccessful launch of a new drug and marketing and sales managers tell their subordinates everything they need to stop doing.

If we are experiencing adversity and feeling the corresponding stress that it induces, we experience auditory exclusion. Our military or athletic teammates often only hear "Shoot," "Pass," or "Call time out." Our corporate teammates are challenged to remember what exactly they are supposed to stop doing rather than what they must start. All teammates react exactly the opposite of what we wanted them to do. This is partly because we may not hear the "don't" part of the command. It is also because in those stressful situations, there are certain words that we are unconsciously waiting for, because they will allow us to take action, which we all want to do. Most importantly, if we are asking our team to stop doing certain things, it means that they have already made a habit of doing those things. As discussed in earlier chapters, it is a challenge to change habits. Cluttering our communication with both what needs to stop and what needs to start makes changing those habits even more difficult.

Never tell a Marine "Don't Shoot" in the middle of a firefight—as soon as he hears a "shh" sound, he is pulling the trigger. "Hold your fire" is much more effective.

Although we may need to stop doing some things to turn around the financial quarter our corporate team may be experiencing, as leaders we need to understand that telling our team what not to do is not helping them figure out what actions to take. Discuss what you need to stop doing, but spend the great majority of your time communicating what to do. It makes remembering it easier. Further, after departing your weekly, nonstressful meeting, one of your salespeople will find themselves in an important, stressful sales meeting. As leaders, are we certain that that salesperson will not confuse what they are supposed to say with what they are not supposed to say? Are we confident that our salesperson will not confuse what they are supposed to do with what they are not supposed to do? Positively communicating helps ensure better outcomes.

Michigan men's basketball faced North Carolina in the 1993 National Championship. Trailing 73–71, Chris Webber, the most famous figure of the vaunted Michigan Fab Five, pulled down a rebound and started down the court. With 20 seconds left, they had plenty of time to set up one last play to take the potential winning shot. The only problem was that they had no timeouts left and could not set up a final play. They would just have to figure one out. As Chris dribbled up the floor he hesitated with the ball and traveled. The referee trailing the play either did not see it or chose not to call it. The UNC bench exploded in outrage. Knowing that he had traveled and almost cost his team the game, we can only imagine the stress this heaped on Chris's shoulders, stress already magnified by the screaming fans, the bright lights, and the ticking clock. As he dribbled by the Michigan bench, the UNC defenders trapped him and pressed him into the corner. In deep trouble, Chris brought his hands together and called a timeout. The problem was that Michigan didn't have any timeouts left. This resulted in a technical foul, which gave UNC two free throws and the ball. This effectively ended the Fab Five's championship hopes. Chris Webber has never spoken publicly about the play. However, sources on the scene have confirmed multiple people screaming, "Don't call timeout! Don't call timeout." Outside of combat, we can't imagine a much more stressful environment than being down by two points in a National Championship basketball game with only a few seconds left on the clock. There could have been countless reasons why Chris Webber called a timeout in that situation. Ensuring the use of positive communication (i.e., "Throw it off his leg!") or some other command telling Chris what to do, instead of what *not* to do, would have guaranteed that auditory exclusion was not among them.

If necessary, discuss what needs to change, but always communicate to your teammates what you want them to do. Regardless of the battlefield, positively communicate.

75

Using a Back Brief

ON EVERY BATTLEFIELD, leaders bring their team together and explain what they need the team to do. They might even draw it up. After they are done, the leader inevitably asks, "Does anyone have any questions?" In our entire careers, we can't remember a single time when a teammate volunteered, "Actually, yes, I do have questions." Instead, everyone shakes their head, mumbles "No," and then runs back onto their battlefield as quickly as possible. The resulting "play" looks absolutely nothing like the play that the leader had communicated, demonstrating that the team did not have a good grasp on it at all, despite their lack of questions when asked if they had any.

To combat this, we recommend using a technique called a back brief. In the military, for any mission we embark upon, we give an operations order, which is often long, detailed, and complicated. When the briefer is done delivering it, instead of asking, "Does anyone have any questions?" he or she utilizes the back brief technique. The briefer will call on various members of the unit to brief back important sections of the operations order.

This does two things. First, it gives the briefer confidence that their message was delivered correctly and that their unit understands what they are doing. Second, it forces the entire unit to stay focused during the brief, knowing that they may be called on afterward. When utilizing the back brief technique, we tend to call on our best and most experienced people. It makes us feel good when they know the answers and can also make us look good in front of our superiors. However, this can be counterproductive because there is always a chance that your newer and less experienced people still do not understand what they are expected to do. Instead, in the Marine Corps, we would make it a point to call on our newest and least cerebral Marines, knowing that if they know the plan, our experienced Marines will as well. There are probably some Marines reading this right now thinking, "Hmmm, so that's why I get called on all the time."

We cannot stress enough to parents, teachers and leaders on every team the importance of utilizing the back brief technique. It will make your team better!

76

Closed-Loop Communication

CLOSED-LOOP COMMUNICATION IS one of the most powerful tools that we can employ throughout our organization. It immediately helps develop trust among teammates, and an unprecedented level of efficiency as we accomplish our mission. It costs us nothing and we can implement it today.

A leader assigns a task and communicates it to a subordinate (closed-loop communication can, and should be, used if a subordinate asks a leader to accomplish a certain task, or between peers, as well). In our example, the subordinate repeats the assigned task back to the leader to ensure that there is no miscommunication on what needs to be accomplished. If the information is correct, the leader responds in the affirmative. If the information has been misunderstood by the subordinate, the leader recommunicates it. This process does two things: it ensures that the information passed is received correctly, and it allows the subordinate to check the message and make sure their leader communicated it correctly. Leader and subordinate discuss and determine if the subordinate is to close the loop on the task prior to its completion or only when it is finished. The subordinate then completes the task. As soon as it is accomplished (or earlier, if requested), the subordinate closes the loop with their leader by confirming it has been accomplished.

Unfortunately, a leader will frequently assign a task or make a request that will take a few days or weeks to accomplish. Often, that communication loop is left open-ended and their subordinate never closes it when the task has been accomplished. Leaving communication open-ended like that can have more than a few deleterious effects. It is possible that the teammate easily accomplished the task, but never reported back to the leader. This can cause wasted time and stress for the leader who wonders about the status of the task and could damage trust on the team. It is also possible that the teammate forgot all about the task and never completed it. If the leader *assumes* the task was completed and acts accordingly, overall mission accomplishment could be at risk.

As discussed earlier, if a task has not been completed, subordinates should still check in and communicate with leaders or peers and update them on their progress (even if little to no progress has been made). If a task is not going to be completed on time, then the assigner of that task should be updated on that fact prior to its deadline.

The Loews Miami Beach Hotel employs nearly 1000 people. During holiday weekends they will have up to 3000 guests. There are countless tasks that must be accomplished on an hourly basis. If Ryan Steele, the hotel manager, spent all his time trying to track down his teammates to check and see if these tasks were accomplished, he wouldn't be able to lead his team. It is a standard on his team that his teammates close the loop with him, or their direct supervisors, on all of their tasks so that Ryan can stay focused on mission accomplishment. In turn, he makes sure to close the loop with his subordinates and superiors alike.

Make a habit of closing the loop in your communications. If you are assigned a task, ensure that you report back throughout its progress, if requested, but always when completed. If the task is taking longer than expected, report that to your leader, along with the timeline for your next update.

Make a habit of closing the loop in your communications. If you are assigned a task ensure that you report back throughout its progress, if requested, but always when completed.

77

Ignoring the Noise

ONE OF THE most common questions that both athletic teams and corporations ask us is "How do we ignore the noise?" The "noise" they are referring to is all of the outside "chatter" that bombards their organization from every direction. As leaders, we are trying to create a world-class culture, but our team members are receiving different, sometimes opposing, messages from the media, friends and family, the public arena, and social media. For example, a head coach tells an athlete that they need to be more selfless. That night, the athlete reads an article on a sports blog saying that the coach is underutilizing them, tweets claim the program is in a downward spiral, and their dad calls them and tells them to "ignore the coach and shoot the ball more." Corporate team members look at their organization's stock price, listen to teammates in other branches about unexpected turnover or downsizing, and even add to the noise by discussing "the latest news" that they just heard. How do we stop all this counterproductive messaging?

We don't. If we spent all our time trying to control every outside source of information, we would not have any time left in the day to do anything else. With smartphones and the internet, the speed and accessibility of information is unparalleled in history, and it is only going to get faster and more accessible. We can't possibly control the messaging that the members of our team are receiving from outside our organization, and trying to do so is a futile waste of time. What we can do is control the messaging that our teammates are receiving from us.

If the head coach decides that the team must focus on their Core Value of selflessness, then an athlete is hearing that message from his head coach, his positional coach, all of his strength coaches, the athletic trainers, the director of football operations, and the head coach's assistant too. Corporate teammates are hearing the same message from their manager that they hear their CEO speak about on CNN. In turn, they will discuss that same message with their direct reports as well.

Too often, though, this doesn't occur, and members of our organization receive as many different messages from inside our team as they do from outside of it. The head coach may preach selflessness, but then our teammate may listen to his positional coach speak about integrity, his strength coach discuss hard work, and then a guest speaker highlight the importance of toughness. When added to everything else the athlete is reading and hearing in the media, on social media, and from friends and family, the head coach's message of selflessness becomes lost in the "noise."

Regardless of the battlefield, if a teammate hears every leader that they interact with that day, week, and month discuss the importance of selflessness, he will much more likely receive messaging that has a meaningful impact and that counteracts all the messaging that he receives from others.

Rather than focusing on trying to stop certain messaging reaching our teammates, we can, and must, make a commitment to focus and communicate our own. What is the mission-essential messaging that our team needs to hear? There are thousands of media outlets and even more social media platforms. We don't control any of them. Rather than worry about their messaging, stay focused on what we do control: our own.

78

Putting the Communication Techniques Together

As a trauma nurse, The Program teammate Shannon Meyer knows how important communication is. Effective communication often had life-or-death ramifications in her daily life. As the officer in charge of a shock trauma platoon, Shannon had to ensure that her entire platoon knew the importance of effective communication. This process began by clearly assigning and communicating roles and responsibilities before a patient ever came in. For example, one of Shannon's teammates might have been responsible for the patient's airway, another would be responsible for medication, another for the crash cart, and so on. Effectively communicating these roles and responsibilities allowed everyone to know exactly what was expected from them before the chaos of a trauma situation hit.

Nurses train to a very high communication standard because they know that the consequences for making a mistake with medication or treatment in a high-stress trauma situation could very well cause the death of a patient. Anytime she was working, Shannon would ensure that she utilized CLAPP while speaking with her team. While working on a trauma patient, the leading nurse might call, "Mike, administer 100mg of ketamine" to sedate the patient. Using closed-loop communication, Mike would respond, "Administering 100mg of ketamine." The leading nurse would respond, "That's correct."

In this situation, too little of the drug would not have the desired effect. Too much could inadvertently kill the patient. The lead nurse could have just yelled, "I need 100mg of ketamine." However, that would run the risk that two people might administer the dose, or that everyone would assume that someone else would do it and the medication is never administered. Using name, command, and volume ensures that everyone knows what they need to do.

Mike, responding and repeating the information back, ensured the dosage given was what the lead nurse wanted. If he disagreed with the dosage, Mike could have also responded, "100mg? Don't you mean 50mg of ketamine?" This could give the lead nurse the opportunity to reassess the communication. At this point, they would still need to close the loop. The lead nurse makes the change and says, "You are correct. Mike, administer 50mg of ketamine." Mike would respond, "Administering 50mg of ketamine." The lead nurse would respond, "Correct."

If the lead nurse wanted to stick with the original dosage, the nurse could reply, "Negative. Administer 100mg of ketamine." To continue the closed-loop process, Mike would still need to reply, "Administering 100mg of Ketamine," and the lead nurse would reply, "Correct," to close the loop.

An emergency room trauma center is extremely stressful and intense. Auditory exclusion is common. This is one of the reasons why we should never hear negative communication. The Risk Management Foundation estimates that 70–80% of medical errors are caused by communication problems. Effective communication is just as key to accomplishing our own missions, regardless of the battlefields on which we fight.

Action Items on Effective Communication

1. Record yourself next time you give a speech or presentation. Which part of CLAPP needs the most work? Do you need to be clear? Louder? More authoritative? Do you need to pause more? Do you need better posture? Pick the one you think needs the most improvement and work on it until you are proficient and ready to attack another part of CLAPP.
2. Make sure you ask yourself and can answer these three questions every single day:

   a. What do I know?

   b. Who else needs to know?

   c. Have I told them?

3. Practice battlefield communication. Anytime you are in an uncontrolled environment (i.e., a volleyball game, the trading floor, a classroom full of third-graders), utilize name, command, and volume. Use the person's name first, tell them what you need them to do, and use the appropriate volume.
4. Use the "back brief" technique whenever possible to ensure that all of your teammates know what they are supposed to do.
5. Make it a habit to eliminate negative communication whenever and wherever possible. Tell your teammates what you need them to do!
6. Great teammates and great team leaders consistently close the loop on all communication. It develops trust throughout an organization.

Saved Round on Effective Communication

Leadership is influence. A leader is someone who has influence, as well as an ability and desire to use it. Leaders maximize their influence through both their actions and, more importantly, their communication. Nowhere is it more critical than in an uncontrolled environment—an environment where there is an enemy

(continued)

Saved Round on Effective Communication (Cont'd)

who wants to kill us, literally in the case of the military and first responder communities or figuratively in the case of athletic and corporate teams.

There is no more confusing and chaotic environment in existence than combat. An inability, or lack of desire, to communicate effectively can destroy confidence and make an already chaotic environment even more so. Chaos breeds chaos. Thankfully, leaders who employ the techniques reviewed in this chapter can provide the complete opposite to their teams on their own chosen battlefields. Calm breeds calm.

Chaos breeds chaos. Calm breeds calm.

The Battle of Najaf was one the most uncontrolled environments in which Mac and his Marines from C Co., 1st Light Armored Battalion, had ever operated. Thankfully, despite having been awake and active for over thirty hours, the Marines were ready for the fight. To make the situation more challenging, Mac's platoon had already been called out once on a false alarm. It would have been natural for the younger Marines to let their guard down, to succumb to a "here we go again" attitude. The fact that complacency did not set in was due to Mac's—and to a much larger part, his subordinate leaders'—commitment to mission accomplishment and taking care of their Marines.

Although the first time they had approached the besieged Iraqi police station it was a proverbial ghost town, that area was now a hornet's nest. As they moved toward the enemy position, bullets were cracking and snapping all around them, some even pinging off the sides of their vehicles. The enemy fire was coming from the Najaf cemetery, but with all the giant and jagged tombstones and multistory crypts, there were too many hiding places to spot any enemy fighters. Mac's senior leaders made the decision to place the Marine forces between the Iraqi police station and the Najaf cemetery, where the enemy fighters were located. Mac and his platoon were given the mission of seizing an important traffic circle in the area.

At this point in the war, the enemy didn't have very accurate indirect fire (mortar, artillery, and rocket) capabilities. However, they knew the importance of the traffic circle and that a U.S. military unit was going to attempt to secure it. Although inaccurate, the bad guys had had the time, and used the opportunity, to "target" the traffic circle prior to the arrival of Mac and his Marines.

Mac's platoon reached the traffic circle and his scouts dismounted from their vehicles to "clear" it (i.e., to make it safe). The world blew up around them. They were immediately battered by a tidal wave of explosions, screams, smoke, and fire everywhere. Most of the nearby Marines were concussed. Mac was paralyzed with fright as he watched one of his best Marines hurled twenty feet by a mortar explosion. When the barrage lifted, Mac knew that he had to give a situation report to his bosses over the radio. He needed to let them know that he was taking indirect fire and that they would be moving to a new position. Every instinct of self-preservation told him to pick up the radio and yell and scream, to cuss like Yosemite Sam, to throw his weapon down, to panic. However, Mac knew that would be the worst thing he could possibly do for his Marines, because chaos breeds chaos, and calm breeds calm. So, counter to his instincts and every desire he possessed, Mac took one deep breath and communicated over the radio. "Palerider, this is Warpig. Taking Fire. Moving Position." He did his absolute best to sound just like he did while training in beautiful Southern California. Everyone is a hero when it is seventy degrees and sunny. Unfortunately, that is not when you need one. You need great teammates and great team leaders when it is not!

As the platoon commander, Mac's personnel actions were limited; he never pulled the trigger on his weapon or threw a grenade. He knew, however, that his ability to communicate effectively would be the difference between a confident, calm, and mission-focused unit of Marines or a fearful, chaotic, and unfocused one. Despite the overwhelming adversity, his ability to communicate effectively would ultimately empower them to accomplish the mission.

Regardless of the battlefield on which we fight, our ability to communicate effectively enables our own teams to do the same.

Acknowledgments

A GREAT COMMANDING OFFICER is imperative for the development and success of subordinates. I would like to thank both of mine, Colonel Jerry Durant and Colonel Robert Coates. Both were men whom I was inspired to follow and emulate. I appreciate their guidance and the high standards that they demanded of me.

As big an impact as both had, it was my platoon sergeants who taught me the most about leadership. I would not be the leader that I am today if I had not been as lucky as I was to have Staff Sergeant George Sanchez and Gunnery Sergeant Tom Dewitt in my life.

I met 2nd Lieutenant Mike Johannes on the first day of the Basic School. He was my roommate. He no longer is, but he remains my best friend. I associate with people who make me better. He has and continues to do so. Thank you.

You don't choose your parents. If I could have, I would have picked the ones I was lucky enough to have been born to. Most parents let their kids grow up. I am so thankful that you *raised* me. To my mom: as a parent, I now appreciate how close you always want your children. I also understand how detrimental that can be. A man is a sum of his experiences. Thank you for telling me to go and have mine. To my dad: thank you for not only telling me, but more importantly, for showing me how to be the best teammate and team leader for my most important team, my family.

Doug Zembiec. WWZD. What Would Zembiec Do? You are still a guiding influence in my life. You will remain as such until I draw my final breath. Not a day goes by that I don't still think about you, Warrior. I miss you.

To my son, Axel, and my daughter, Anastasia: if I have accomplished anything in my life, none of it compares to being your father. It is the greatest joy I have ever had and you are both my (and your mom's) greatest accomplishments. You have both made me better and continue to do so every day in countless ways. Thank you for being my son and daughter. Thank you even more for being such great teammates.

To my wife, Melissa: I am sorry for the mistakes that I have made throughout our long relationship. I appreciate you for not only sticking *by* me, I appreciate you for always *supporting* me. We accomplish nothing in our lives as individuals. Everything we accomplish is as a member of a team. No team is more important to me than our family, and I wouldn't want, nor could I have, a better teammate and team leader than you. I love you with my whole heart and appreciate you even more.

Finally, thank you to all the Marines with whom I had the pleasure of serving. In some way, you each had an everlasting impact on me. Outside of Husband and Daddy, Marine is still my most cherished title.

—Eric Kapitulik

As Marines we often speak about "standing on the shoulders of giants." I have had the honor and privilege of knowing more than a few giants in my life. It is only by standing on their shoulders that I have been able to succeed.

My first battlefield was the football field, and Terry Hennigan at Irvine High School and Mike Browne at Tufts University, taught me to be tough, humble, and loyal.

I served on countless actual battlefields during my time in the Marine Corps. Every single Marine with whom I served had an impact on me, many of whom I literally owe my life to—in particular Trent Gibson, Gil Juarez, Jason Smith, John Mayer, Dave Lewis, Jason Soucy, and Matt Chase. You all impacted my life differently, but all moved me in the right direction. I only hope this book is an accurate reflection of the lessons you taught me.

The first Marine I ever met was my father, John MacDonald Jr. He has guided and influenced me throughout my life. I'm proud that we share the title United States Marine. I'm even prouder that we share the same name. My mom, Elaine, was, and is, every bit as tough as my Marine father. Through countless moves and cross-country drives, my mom taught me to be resilient and to always maintain a positive attitude. My sister, Kate, despite being a far superior athlete to me, showed me what it means to be a great teammate. I love you all.

My wife, Maria, is the love of my life and has done an amazing job of leading our family. I believe that through hard work and preparation we make our own luck. But, in this case, I am so lucky that you came into my life. I love you. My son, Johnny, and daughter, Sasha, keep me going and I can barely remember what my life was like before they came into it. Singing the Marines' Hymn to them as they fall asleep is always the best part of my day.

—Jake MacDonald

Eric and Mac would also like to thank:

Our editor, Vicki Adang. This book flat out would not exist without your guidance, counsel, and most importantly your patience.

Zach Schisgal and his team at Wiley Publishing. Thank you for putting your trust and faith in two first-time authors. Your advice along the way was, and is, always spot on and appreciated.

The Program team. We feel so fortunate to be able to call these men and women teammates. In particular, we want to thank Ghislaine Stonnaker. She was our proofreader, research assistant, sounding board, and shoulder to cry on, among other varied and crucial roles. Her contributions to this book may not be visible to the reader, but her influence is in every word and page.

Special thanks to Kylie Knight, Ohio State women's soccer captain, class of 2019, who helped track down so much of the data used in the book. She was invaluable. We would be remiss if we didn't also recognize Jamie Haines. Thank you so much for taking care of "the little things"—like grammar and punctuation!

Finally, we would like to thank all military veterans and those currently serving, as well as the emergency first-responder community. We live in peace and prosperity with individual freedoms unlike any other country in the world. Thank you for providing it.

About the Authors

ERIC KAPITULIK WAS born and raised in Thompson, Connecticut, and attended Pomfret Preparatory School, where he was a three-sport varsity athlete. Upon graduating, he attended the United States Naval Academy. While there, he was a four-year varsity letter winner and played on three NCAA Division I lacrosse tournament teams. During his junior year, Eric received the Lieutenant (junior-grade) Frank McKeone Award, given to the Navy player who most demonstrated spirit and sportsmanship and who served as the unsung hero. Eric was also named Navy's Most Outstanding Defenseman and received North-South All Star honors his senior year at the academy. He graduated in 1995 and went on to serve as both an Infantry Officer and Special Operations Officer with 1st Force Reconnaissance Company, 1st Marine Division. He left active duty after eight years of service and graduated from the University of Chicago Graduate School of Business in 2005.

Eric has been extensively involved with the Force Reconnaissance Scholarship Fund, which he established for the children of six Marines who died in a helicopter crash while serving under his command. Since 1999, he has been helping to raise funds, and has done so through public speaking engagements covering "Leadership and Attacking Adversity," and through participation in Iron Man triathlons and other ultra-endurance races around the world. In addition to finishing eight Iron Man triathlons, Eric has competed in numerous marathons, the Canadian Death Race ultramarathon, the Eco Challenge, and the American Birkebeiner Ski Marathon, and was a competitor on the Outdoor Life Network's "Global Extremes Challenge."

Eric is also an avid high-altitude mountaineer. He has summited five of the Seven Summits (the highest peaks on the seven continents): Mount Kilimanjaro, Mount McKinley, Mount Aconcagua, Mount Elbrus, and most recently, Mount Everest.

Eric sits on the board of directors for the Massachusetts Soldier's Legacy Fund and is the founder and president of The Program LLC, a team-building and leadership development company for collegiate and professional athletes and corporate teams.

Jake MacDonald graduated in 2000 from Tufts University with a degree in English. He was a four-year starter and captain of the varsity football team his senior year. After graduating, Jake was commissioned as an officer in the United States Marine Corps. While on active duty, he completed two combat tours to Iraq as a Light Armored Reconnaissance Platoon Commander. He continued to serve his country as a Major in the Marine Corps Reserves and deployed to Afghanistan as a Scout Sniper Platoon Commander. Jake has received multiple awards for combat valor as well as a Purple Heart after being wounded in action.